MW00638057

HEILONGJIANG

• Harbin

BLIC

JILIN

• Changchun

MONGOL AUTONOMOUS REGION (Inner Mongolia)

• Shenyang

LIAONING

NORTH KOREA

Hohhot   HEBEI

Beijing ■   • Tangshan • Dalian

Tianjin•

SOUTH KOREA   JAPAN

Taiyuan

Taigu   SHANDONG ▲ Lao Shan

Jishan • Linfen   Jinan • Qingdao

NXIA

Yanan

SHANXI   ▲ Tai Shan

Huangling • Wanrong • Jincheng

• Qishan

Xian •   Luoyang • Kaifeng   JIANGSU

R BASIN ▲ Hua Shan   HENAN   ANHUI

SHAANXI   Hefei • • Nanjing

▲ Wudang Shan   Mao Shan • Shanghai

HUBEI   Hangzhou• ▲ Putuo Shan

• Wuhan   Shaoxing • Ningbo

• Chongqing   JIANGXI   ZHEJIANG

• Nanchang • Wenzhou

• Changsha

▲ Heng Shan

UIZHOU   HUNAN   Pacific Ocean

• Guiyang   FUJIAN • Fuzhou

• Guilin ▲ Jiuyi Shan   • Taipei

TAIWAN

• Xiamen • Chia I

GUANGXI   GUANGDONG × Shantou • Chiahsien

AUTONOMOUS

REGION   Tainan•

• Nanning   • Guangzhou   Tungkang

Hong Kong

Macau

South China Sea

HAINAN   THE PHILIPPINES

Chinese Mythological Gods

TITLES IN THE SERIES

Arts of the Tang Court
PATRICA EICHENBAUM KARETZKY

At the Chinese Table
T.C. LAI

At the Japanese Table
RICHARD HOSKING

The Cheongsam
HAZEL CLARK

China's Muslims
MICHAEL DILLON

China's Walled Cities
RONALD G. KNAPP

Chinese Almanacs
RICHARD J. SMITH

Chinese Bridges
RONALD G. KNAPP

Chinese Classical Furniture
GRACE WU BRUCE

The Chinese Garden
JOSEPH CHO WANG

The Chinese House
RONALD G. KNAPP

Chinese Jade
JOAN HARTMAN-GOLDSMITH

Chinese Maps
RICHARD J. SMITH

Chinese Musical Instruments
ALAN R. THRASHER

Chinese Mythological Gods
KEITH G. STEVENS

Chinese New Year
PATRICIA BJAALAND WELCH

Chinese Painting
T.C. LAI

Chinese Paper Offerings
RODERICK CAVE

Chinese Snuff Bottles
ROBERT KLEINER

Chinese Tomb Figurines
ANN PALUDAN

The Forbidden City
MAY HOLDSWORTH

Japanese Cinema: An Introduction
DONALD RICHIE

The Japanese Kimono
HUGO MUNSTERBERG

Japanese Musical Instruments
HUGH DE FERRANTI

Korean Musical Instruments
KEITH HOWARD

Korean Painting
KEITH PRATT

Macau
CÉSAR GUILLÉN-NUÑEZ

Mandarin Squares: Mandarins and their Insignia
VALERY M. GARRETT

The Ming Tombs
ANN PALUDAN

Modern Chinese Art
DAVID CLARKE

New Chinese Cinema
KWOK-KAN TAM &
WIMAL DISSANAYAKE

Old Kyoto
JOHN LOWE

Old Shanghai
BETTY PEH-T'I WEI

Peking Opera
COLIN MACKERRAS

Temples of the Empress of Heaven
JOSEPH BOSCO & PUAY-PENG HO

Traditional Chinese Clothing
VALERY M. GARRETT

Series Editors, China Titles:
NIGEL CAMERON, SYLVIA FRASER-LU

Chinese Mythological Gods

KEITH G. STEVENS

Oxford University Press is a department of the University of Oxford.
It furthers the University's objective of excellence in research, scholarship,
and education by publishing worldwide in

Oxford New York

Athens Auckland Bangkok Bogotá Buenos Aires Cape Town
Chennai Dar es Salaam Delhi Florence Hong Kong Istanbul Karachi
Kolkata Kuala Lumpur Madrid Melbourne Mexico City Mumbai Nairobi
Paris São Paulo Shanghai Singapore Taipei Tokyo Toronto Warsaw

with associated companies in Berlin Ibadan

Oxford is a registered trade mark of Oxford University Press

Published in the United States
by Oxford University Press Inc., New York

© Oxford University Press 2001

First published 2001
This impression (lowest digit)
1 3 5 7 9 10 8 6 4 2

British Library Cataloguing in Publication Data
available

Library of Congress Cataloging-in-Publication Data
available

ISBN 0-19-591990-4

Printed in Hong Kong
Published by Oxford University Press (China) Ltd
18th Floor, Warwick House East, Taikoo Place, 979 King's Road, Quarry Bay
Hong Kong

Contents

Acknowledgements   *vi*

1   Chinese Mythological Gods and Demigods:
    An Overview   1

2   Deities of Fate and Destiny   8

3   The Creation of the Universe   25

4   Prehistory and the Legendary Rulers   35

5   The Three Sage Kings   43

6   Mythical Deities of Popular Legend   49

7   Daoist Deities of Nature, Agriculture, and
    Natural Phenomena   59

8   Tutelary Gods and the Gods of the Underworld   67

9   Mythical Deities Revealed during
    the Last Millennium   73

    Chronology   76

    Selected Bibliography   77

    Index   79

Acknowledgements

WITH HAPPY MEMORIES of those who individually have accompanied me on trips to Chinese temples on the mainland of China, in Taiwan, and South-East Asia: My wife, daughters, and grandchildren, as well as Judith, Julie, and Jeremy, Ines and Hubert, Jenny, Geoff, and Dave, Pat and Lindsay, Helga, Belinda, Gilda, Rachel, Kirsty and Paul, and our intrepid cab driver, Wu Shucui, who drove us over the years for many a thousand miles through five northern provinces of China.

All photographs, bar two, were taken by myself during our travels. For these two, I am particularly grateful to Jennifer Welch for her illustrations; the rare shot of Xi Wangmu, and especially for her unique image of Chang E.

I am also extremely grateful to Carey Vail for her expertise, and for the dedication and care she has taken in the editing of this work.

1

Chinese Mythological Gods and Demigods:
An Overview

MYTH IS GENERALLY an attempt to provide a logical explanation for the great imponderables of our world system—the creation of the universe, the causes of drought and flood, pestilence, plagues of locusts, and the hereafter. Legends, on the other hand, are often based, usually flimsily, on true experiences or actual people who lived long ago. Peasants from all lands have formulated their own, humanly intelligible theories of how the universe came about, how it works, and how it came to be populated with powerful personalities and deities.

Chinese myths describe the lives and times of beings that took part in the creation and development of the universe, and the legendary beings of mankind's protohistory. Only a few of these beings, however, have been revered and worshipped on Chinese altars as gods and demigods, and it is these few who feature in this book. The lives and legends of historical heroes whose images are so frequently seen on Chinese altars, such as Guan Di, the God of Loyalty, fall outside the remit of this work in spite of their apotheoses and claim to divine status.

Chinese social and moral conduct has been largely governed by Confucianism, a philosophy with a marked antagonism to the concept of gods and the myriad spirits. Chinese religious beliefs, however, have been dominated by Daoism and Buddhism, the former teachings embodying the mystic, liturgical, or transcendental teaching of the Dao, or Way, and the latter faith introduced from India nearly two thousand years ago. In addition, there is a widespread popular

1

religion—sometimes called folk religion—which includes not only the deities of Buddhism and Daoism, but also the legendary demigods and the spirits of apotheosized divinities, that is, the spirits of historical heroes, meritorious officials, and local worthies whose individual powers provide protection and succour for devotees. All three categories that make up popular religion—the mythic gods, the legendary demigods, and the deified human divinities—were referred to by Christian missionaries as heathen gods or idols. Other Westerners simply grouped them all together as 'gods'.

There is not always a straightforward division between mythological gods and the legendary demigods. Gods, despite being represented in human form on altars, never had a human existence, whereas the demigods are legendary deified humans who lived during the dawn of history; it is not possible to accurately date their human lives. The first mythological deities were the gods of the universe, or gods of pre-creation, followed by the gods of creation.

Next came the legendary heroes of prehistory. They are the demigods, the sage emperors, and their ministers who, through the mists of time, are regarded as the founders of Chinese culture. They may have been individual humans with unbelievable longevity though, more likely, they were the embodiment of dynasties.

Finally we have local urban and rustic mythical beings, non-humans who as recently as 100 years ago descended to China from the heavens. Cults surrounding such local gods have spread throughout their home provinces and even across swathes of China. Others have not been seen beyond the village that they honoured with their presence.

Although the mythical deities of China were generally not the monster-slayers found in alternative traditions, a small number of Chinese mythical heroes were. Some native

Chinese mythical deities, such as Bei Di, the Northern Emperor, and Yang Jian, a god of popular religion, are accompanied by tractable animals, which are their associated creatures: snake, tortoise, and dog. Other deities imported into China by, for example, Tantric Buddhism, take the form of monster-headed human deities.

The gods taking part in the cataclysmic events of the creation range from the actual creators of the world to those who later taught mankind agriculture and social behaviour. Also, there are those who saved mankind from landmark disasters, such as the epochal floods caused by a rupture in the dome of the sky and the lesser floods of the annual cycle. These and all the other events leading eventually to the stabilization of Chinese civilization are recorded in myth and legend, with two major historico-legendary tales in particular indelibly influencing and colouring the beliefs of popular religion.

The first of these tales, and the most influential of all recorded stories, is the *Fengshen Yanyi* (Deification of the Gods). This romance of the Ming dynasty (1368–1644), which can be read as an unsophisticated version of history, addresses the moral and philosophical question of the origins of the gods, and describes a great many of the legendary deities. It is a highly colourful account of the decline of the Shang dynasty during the twelfth century BC, with its depraved, dissolute, and brutal ruler, under the spell of a beautiful concubine, and the struggle by the vassal state of Zhou to overthrow it. The work standardized many myths and legends into a continuous story which, since its compilation, has been the wellspring of Chinese popular knowledge about the celestial and underworld deities. It became the fount from which tea shop storytellers, temple custodians, and god carvers took their inspiration, as well as the form and style of statues and images. The *Fengshen Yanyi* has an overlay of Buddhism, despite this religion only reaching China a further thousand years after the overthrow of the Shang and the establishment of the Zhou dynasty.

The struggle between the Shang and the Zhou is described in gory detail, with humans and deities waging unrestricted warfare using thunderbolts, poisonous gasses, and magic fans. Armies are annihilated by wizardry; bizarre and fantastic magic weapons are deployed by both sides, leading to the eventual defeat of the Shang, the suicide of the ruler, and the death of his concubine. It takes place during the era when the Chinese in the Yellow River Basin were emerging from prehistory. Dates of the drama vary from 1050 to 1127 BC, but the final act is well known to all Chinese: the canonization of the heroes on both sides of the conflict. Jiang Ziya, the heroic prime minister of the victorious Zhou (see Chapter 2), became responsible for handing out honours deifying the human heroes, with both victors and vanquished being awarded posts in the celestial hierarchy. Images of many of these heroes, now deities in their own right, can still be seen today on altars, each fulfilling his responsibility and specific role as the God of Wealth, the God of Health, a patron deity, and so forth.

The Chinese of antiquity superimposed the structure of their dynastic government upon their celestial pantheon, in a realm where both individual euhemerized heroes and worthies, and groups of mythical deities took up their hierarchical positions. The *Fengshen Yanyi* also describes in detail the Celestial Ministries that run the spiritual bureaucracy. Each ministry or board is responsible for either remedial action—the Board of Epidemics, for example, protects people from the evils of disease—or for the betterment of society, such as the Board of Literature. There are in all some dozen ministries: the Ministry of Medicine, the Waters, Time, Fire, War, Finance, Exorcisms, Public Works, Thunder, and Agriculture, and even a Ministry of the Five Sacred Mountains.

Although the specific heavenly hierarchies vary from community to community, China's celestial pantheon remains much as it has been for centuries and forms an integral part of popular religion.

The second major tale to so profoundly influence Chinese popular religion is the *Xiyou Ji* (Journey to the West), a fanciful sixteenth-century account based loosely on the historical pilgrimage of Xuanzang, a Buddhist monk. Xuanzang was a genuine pilgrim who travelled to India during the early part of the seventh century. There he studied for some seventeen years before returning to China with sacred books, images, and icons relating to Buddhism. In the novel he is escorted by the Monkey King, Sun Wukong, who usurps the leading role and becomes the hero. Monkey is an exotic character whose fabulous and magical adventures during the journey frequently saved the pilgrim monk and his precious religious treasures. While the real story of the monk's pilgrimage must have been exciting enough, the adventures related in the novel describe in great detail the activities of the recalcitrant Monkey King, together with two other minor mythical characters, Pig and a labouring monk, Sha, who helped protect and carry the Buddhist scriptures (Fig. 1.1). The story, a satire of traditional Chinese society, portrays an interrelationship between the various religions and beliefs, with Buddhist deities decidedly successful in controlling the scallywag Monkey King, and Daoist deities failing miserably to do so.

Throughout China, images of most major deities are portrayed in splendid robes, seated, with stern, impassive

1.1 The Monkey King, Sun Wukong, leads the famous group of pilgrims from the *Xiyou Ji* (Journey to the West), a sixteenth-century account of the great pilgrimage to India. They are Xuanzang, the Buddhist monk, Zhu Bajie (Pig, or Piggy), and the monk and porter, Sha. Bukit Timah, Singapore.

faces glaring out at terrestrial mankind. Mythological deities before the advent of Huang Di, the Yellow Emperor, however, are usually depicted dressed in skins or, more frequently, skirts and boleros of leaves. The logic behind this is obvious: they lived on earth before the time of the Yellow Emperor, who first devised clothing for humans.

To this day, Chinese devotees seek personal assistance and guidance from the deities, including direct aid from or through the mythical gods and legendary demigods on temple altars. The popular appeal of mythological gods rests on the belief that they possess sufficient 'seniority' to have ready access to the supreme deity, the mythical Yu Huang Dadi, the Jade Emperor (see Chapter 6), to make a personal appeal on behalf of the devotee.

Statues, paintings, prints, and embroidered images of mythological deities can be found in Daoist temples and monasteries, though occasionally they will also be seen in the temples of popular religion. In daily life, the gods and demigods, be they mythological beings or simply deified heroes, are comforters, guardians, guides, and physicians—devotees have learned their histories and the huge body of stories about them through oral tradition.

China, as vast and diverse as the whole of Europe, is far from being a monolithic unity. Many distinct ethnic groups have their own myths, legends, and religious traditions within their own cultures, though certain features transcend regional boundaries. What we tend to regard as Chinese civilization developed within a limited area along the Yellow River Basin, and over the millennia it has spread and absorbed the myths and legends of others. China's early civilization developed along the fertile alluvial plains in southern Shanxi province, where a stable agrarian society emerged some six or seven thousand years ago. It then slowly extended across the rest of what is today the country's central and southern provinces. With this expansion went China's gods as well.

2

Deities of Fate and Destiny

OVER THE CENTURIES, myths and legends of the lives of China's historical figures, heroes, worthies, bandits and revolutionaries, sovereigns, and commoners have become mythologized, largely through generations of tea shop storytellers. Fantasy has been wedded to historico-fictional tales to create a world of heroes and supernatural characters.

Jiang Ziya

Jiang Ziya (Plate 1), a major legendary Daoist deity, is today regarded as the commanding general of all celestial forces and, as such, a powerful protector of homes and shops. Stories about Jiang are involved and complex. Some claim him to be of peasant stock, a man who during the twelfth century BC rose to become a general renowned for his bravery. Others claim he was a Daoist philosopher and seeker after immortality.

Most storytellers, however, affirm that Jiang Ziya started out as an ineffectual trader trying to satisfy his wife's extravagant demands. He was eventually introduced to the Shang-dynasty court and its evil king, Zhou Xin (Plate 2), who gave him a high position. Jiang antagonised Zhou Xin's concubine, Da Ji, by destroying one of her vampire friends, who had disguised herself as a human to share with the evil queen the flesh and blood of slaughtered victims. Jiang was being taken away to be executed outside the palace but managed to escape and finally appeared back home, where he bore the full fury of his wife, as she had been enjoying the perks of the wife of a high official. He explained that he had no intention of returning to the palace—the fortunes of the evil Zhou Xin of the Shang had a further twenty years to run—and instead went to spend his days fishing.

After the defeat of the Shang by the Zhou dynasty, Jiang was encouraged to return to court to serve the victorious ruler and eventually became prime minister. The tyrannical Shang king died within his palace, engulfed in a fire (Plate 3) started on his orders after he realized that the war was lost, and having seen the decapitated head of his licentious, inhuman concubine, Da Ji. She had been sentenced to death, but retained enough of her beauty and charm that none could be found to deal her a fatal stroke. At length Jiang covered his face, stepped forward, and despatched the enchantress.

At the end of the Shang–Zhou wars, Jiang presided at the great Investiture, or canonization ceremony, during which he awarded celestial posts and titles to the heroes and worthies who died on both sides during the conflict. Yuanshi Tianzun, one of the three supreme deities of Daoism (see Chapter 3), issued the sacred mandate to Jiang Ziya, who then read it out to the spirits of the dead heroes and ordered that they should be worshipped by the people as protectors of the nation and its people, and that they should regulate the wind, rain, and natural forces for the benefit of all. They were authorized to reward good deeds and punish the wicked. At the time, heaven was in turmoil because no one was in charge. Jiang planned to appoint himself supreme deity, the Jade Emperor, but as we shall see in Chapter 6, he was foiled, whereupon he made himself chief minister of the spirit world and brought heaven back to its former state before it had fallen into upheaval and confusion.

Yang Jian

Yang Jian, a god of popular religion, has a background complicated by irreconcilable beliefs and identifications. One school of thought regards Yang Jian to be the same as Er Lang, the Second Born, or perhaps a nephew of the Jade Emperor. Another school believes Yang Jian and Er Lang are two discrete deities. Whatever the case, it seems that Yang Jian was awarded the posthumous title of Er Lang, and his fame has spread especially among devotees in southern Chinese communities. They regard him as one of the legendary heroes of the *Fengshen Yanyi*, who helped Jiang Ziya overthrow the Shang dynasty, and pray to him as a benevolent deity who can help those in trouble and need. Yang Jian also drives away demons and wards off demonic influences.

The *Fengshen Yanyi* includes a number of detailed stories and adventures about Er Lang (Plate 4). One tale tells how Er Lang and his dog helped to capture Sun Wukong, the Monkey King, also known as Qitian Dasheng, after he had made heaven too hot for himself. The dog eventually became a dragon and entered a well in the temple courtyard at Guankou in Sichuan province; the well has never since run dry. In the same courtyard sick people would rub themselves on the cast-iron image of the dog to obtain a cure for either themselves or their dogs. Another popular story tells of a Beijing butcher who, noticing that the best bits of meat disappeared from his shop overnight, set a trap and caught the guilty party, a dog, and stabbed it. He then followed the trail of blood until he arrived at the nearby temple and came upon a gash in the side of the image of Er Lang's dog. His business quickly failed. Such canine adventures have led to Er Lang being regarded as the patron deity of dogs.

Yet another tale describes how a beautiful concubine of an emperor, neglected and frustrated by her lord, knelt before an image of the handsome Er Lang and wished for a lover as tall and as handsome as he. The temple keeper, hearing her wish, dressed himself as Er Lang, entered her suite, and made passionate love to her. This he frequently repeated until word got about and an investigation was made. The story ends with the execution of the temple keeper and the concubine.

Li Jing Tianwang

Li Jing Tianwang, General Li Jing, is one of the Twenty-four Heavenly Generals, or Kings, the powerful group of protective deities who command celestial armies. Li Jing was immortalized for his bravery and influence during the legendary wars. He fought for the victorious Zhou, helped overthrow the Shang dynasty, and became a senior minister

2.1 Li Jing Tianwang, one of the Twenty-four Heavenly Generals, and a guardian of the Jade Emperor. At the Longmen Caves he stands as Lord of the North, with pagoda on upturned palm. Longmen, Henan.

11

of heaven following the mass deification at the Investiture. Li, a guardian of the Jade Emperor, is revered for his powers as a destroyer of demons, and some also claim that he was incarnated as Li Bing, a third-century BC flood-controlling minister in Sichuan. He also fills several other roles: father of Nazha San Taizi, or Li Nazha; Lord of the North, one of the Buddhist Four Guardians of the Gates of Heaven; and head of the Yaksha, tamed demons who are the strong, brave spirit soldiers of the celestial armies. Daoist priests offer incense to Li Jing's image during funeral ceremonies for fellow priests; Chinese soldiers in imperial China used to pray before him for protection prior to battle.

Images of General Li portray him as a soldier bearing a small golden pagoda or stupa on the upturned palm of his outstretched hand (Fig. 2.1). Legends abound about Li and his pagoda. One suggests that it is a prison in which he incarcerates the demons he captures, yet another that it is the support of heaven—should it slip, heaven would collapse.

Nazha San Taizi

Folk tales echo the feud between Li Jing and his recalcitrant son, Li Nazha, also known as Nazha San Taizi, the Third Prince (Plate 5). This third son of Li Jing was despatched down to earth by the Jade Emperor in order to subdue the demons raging through the world. He is a powerful deity of popular religion, an exorcising spirit renowned for exploits described in great detail in the *Fengshen Yanyi*. But Nazha is also the *enfant terrible* of Chinese mythology.

He grew up full of mischief and he comes across as a scallywag and a troublemaker. He caused untold aggravation and exasperation, in particular when at the age of seven he unintentionally killed one of the sons of Long Wang, the

Dragon King (see Chapter 7), thus starting a major quarrel involving the Jade Emperor and Nazha's parents. He persisted in being a problem child and eventually committed suicide, returning his body to his parents. Nazha's mother secretly erected a shrine to him, where his spirit proved efficacious. This led his furious father to have the shrine destroyed.

Nazha's spiritual powers, enhanced by devotees' prayers, were recognized by Taiyi Zhenren (an immortal whose patron was Taiyi Jiuku Tianzun, see Chapter 8), so he reconstituted the youth from a lotus flower and brought him back to life. Li Nazha carried on as uncontrollably as ever, yet as time passed he came under the benevolent spell of Taiyi Zhenren and took part in the great mythical battles leading to the overthrow of the Shang. Eventually Li Jing became reconciled with his wayward son, and in the end Wen Shu Tianzun (Manjusri), one of China's four great Buddhist saviours, presented General Li with his golden pagoda to commemorate the occasion, and to symbolize the permanency of the reconciliation.

To Chinese peasants, the numerous legends surrounding the life of Nazha are probably better known than recent imperial history. He is one of several Chinese deities whose identity has evolved from an original Hindu deity: Nata, the third son of Vaisravana (Lord of the North), to Nazha via Buddhism, to Chinese popular religion. Although Nazha and his father, Li Jing, were both originally Indian deities, few Chinese would believe or even accept this to be so.

Images of Nazha show him as a barefoot, muscular youth standing with one foot perched on a 'wind and fire wheel', which enables him to fly through the air like the wind. He holds a magic spear or trident in his right hand, and a large gold or jade 'bracelet' (or ring) in his left. The latter is a powerful and effective throwing weapon known as a 'heaven and earth bracelet', which can kill hundreds as it speeds through the air. It can also be used to pin a foe to the ground by the neck, rendering him immobile. His supernatural powers and other gifts, including his fire wheel and bracelet, were bestowed upon him by his master, Taiyi Zhenren.

In a temple in Jishan in Shanxi province, dedicated to the first king of the victorious Zhou dynasty, images of Nazha and Er Lang flank an image of Jiang Ziya.

Generals Heng and Ha

Generals Heng and Ha, described in the *Fengshen Yanyi* as human generals in the armies of the Shang-dynasty 'tyrant Zhou Wang' (Zhou Xin), are portrayed with partially open mouths, one wider than the other, reminding us that these two fought with secret weapons. One blew a deadly yellow gas from his mouth with a 'ha!', the other snorted a white beam of light from each nostril (or from his third eye) with a 'heng!', which evaporated enemies. Thus they were colloquially known as Ha the Blower and Heng the Snorter.

Both had learned tricks from a magician, in particular the snorting of deadly rays and yellow gas, and after numerous escapades, battles, victories, and defeats, the two found themselves on opposing sides in a duel to the death. They both died and were later canonized by Jiang Ziya, who bestowed upon them the office of Guardians of the Gates of Buddha. Their images nowadays flank the entrance to a number of temples in Yunnan and Jiangxi, and in many places in northern China from Beijing to Xian. They are strong, muscular figures dressed in armour, and hold either a spear or a magic sword; they stand guard with ogre-like features, poised to strike. The left hand guardian (when facing the entrance gate) is the open-mouthed Ha, usually portrayed with a blue or vermilion face, and on the right stands Heng, with closed or partially opened mouth and a green face, which in some temples is charcoal-coloured.

Qitian Dasheng

Qitian Dasheng, Great Sage the Equal of Heaven, is the fabulous and incorrigible Sun Wukong, the Monkey King,[1] whose adventures have thrilled the Chinese for centuries (Fig. 2.2). Few will not have listened in fascination to the legends about the wily ape with his magic club, which can be short enough to carry behind his ear or large enough to destroy groups of enemies at a blow.

The Monkey King is a powerful saint, one who is known to be both helpful yet wilful, both artful yet unpredictable. Many Chinese regard him as a defender and protector of the

2.2 Qitian Dasheng, Great Sage the Equal of Heaven, known colloquially as Sun Wukong, the Monkey King, holds one of the peaches of immortality that he stole from the Peach Garden in the Western Heavens. Author's personal collection.

15

Buddhist doctrine; his image, however, is normally seen in temples of popular religion, and only rarely on Buddhist altars, though occasionally he might appear in a temple side hall. Expectant mothers, gamblers, and the sick in particular pray to him as a major spirit-medium deity. He is able to control demons, transport himself anywhere in a flash, assume any shape or form, and can bestow wealth and health on devotees.

Wen Chang Dijun

Wen Chang Dijun, the mythical Lord Wen Chang, is the patron of the literati—revered by hopeful students and scholars—even though most foreigners assume Confucius to be the God of Literary Tradition and Literature. Wen Chang's status as a state deity highlights his importance; in former times he was officially sanctioned by the imperial bureaucracy, perhaps under the seal of the emperor himself. Aspiring scholars believed his role was to supervise the filling of official posts, promotions within the bureaucracy, and maintenance of records and registers of scholars. It was usual for state officials to render worship at the vernal and autumnal equinoxes. Wen Chang, together with Confucius, records the details of the life and death of all scholars, and any plea or application to change the length of a scholar's life must be authorized by both. Wen Chang is accompanied on altars by a group of assistants, the best known being Kui Xing, an apotheosized scholar and the deity propitiated by students immediately prior to examinations.

Tai Sui

Tai Sui (Plate 6), Ruler of the Year, and president of the Celestial Ministry of Time, was one of the 356 deities canonized by Jiang Ziya at the Investiture. He is the god of the cycle of sixty years, a deity honoured at the beginning of spring by the official class in imperial China, as well as by Daoists. One of the fiercest gods in the pantheon, he must be placated whenever the ground is disturbed for any reason.

Tai Sui today is a stellar deity of popular folk religion, an arbiter of the destiny of mankind and worshipped to avert disaster. Several factors are believed to control human lives, among which is astrology; geomancy,[2] however, is not included. Each year within the recurring cycle of sixty years is ruled by one of the subsidiary Tai Sui. The date and hour of birth of mortals are matched to the movements of Tai Sui across the constellations, information about which is given in an almanac, thereby obtaining the auspicious and inauspicious dates for most social functions, such as weddings, travel, starting a business, launching a ship, or burying the dead. Devotees wishing to seek Tai Sui's aid place spirit-money offerings under the image in the group of sixty that represents the year of their birth.

Tai Sui, literally 'Great Year', is also known by his personal name, Yin Jiao, or Marshal Yin, which reflects his canonization in the *Fengshen Yanyi*. Here he is portrayed as both a good human and a very ugly demonic deity with an indigo face and long, protruding fangs. He was born a lump of formless flesh, which so horrified his father, Zhou Xin, the evil king of the Shang dynasty, that he ordered it to be abandoned outside the city walls. The lump was recognized as an immortal, the caul split open, and the infant removed. The child was nursed and brought up by one of the Eight Immortals—a group of eight human heroes and heroines who gained immortality through meditation and the performance of good deeds—and when he came of age he was told of his birth and the death of his mother. She had been defenestrated on the orders of her husband, Zhou Xin, as punishment for bearing such a 'monster'. Yin Jiao was determined to destroy not only his father but also the imperial concubine, Da Ji, who had brought about the death of Yin's mother by her false accusation that the queen was a fox-demon in disguise and had therefore given birth to a freak. The goddess Tian Fei presented Yin with two magic weapons: a gold club and a battleaxe. After the great conflict between the forces of the Shang and Zhou, Yin helped destroy the concubine.

Yin Jiao is also referred to as Yin Tianjun (Yin the Heavenly Lord), one of the Twenty-four Heavenly Lords. At the end of the *Fengshen Yanyi*, Yin Jiao, having been sent by heaven to bring calamity to King Zhou Xin because of his evil ways, volunteered to be the executioner of both his father and the wicked mistress, Da Ji. He was later proclaimed Prince Jingming.

Ershiba Xiuxing

Ershiba Xiuxing, the Twenty-eight Constellations, are a group of stellar gods, each with a title and specific role. The role and number of these mythological celestial spirits can change with different traditions, though generally all agree that in early China the visible stars were divided into twenty-eight constellations, with seven in each of the four directions. Images of the twenty-eight are very rarely seen on altars. A superb, possibly unique grouping of all twenty-eight images lines a side hall in the Jade Emperor Temple near Jincheng in southern Shanxi province.

Xuantian Shangdi

Xuantian Shangdi, Supreme Lord of the Dark Heavens (Fig. 2.3), is known by a number of titles, which can be

18

confusing for the unwary. He is possibly best known to foreigners as Bei Di, Emperor of the North or the Northern Emperor, and in much of China, particularly in the north, and in parts of Taiwan, as Zhenwu, the True Warrior.

Bei Di is an awesome exorcist, a cult deity within folk religion, a stellar god, and one of the most powerful ministers of the Jade Emperor. He is nearly always depicted with the Snake and Tortoise, both celestial officers under his command, former demons that were conquered by him.[3]

The great popularity of the Northern Emperor has rested for centuries on devotees' belief in the mighty magical powers with which he suppresses demonic forces. According to his devotees, the hordes of malevolent and dangerous evil spirits roaming the earth from the Underworld can only be held in check and destroyed by the Northern Emperor's large force of spirit-soldiers, organized into spirit armies under the Thirty-six Celestial Generals, Sanshiliu Tianjiang.

2.3 Xuantian Shangdi, Supreme Lord of the Dark Heavens, is also known as Bei Di, the Emperor of the North, one of the Jade Emperor's most powerful ministers. Mao Shan, Jiangsu.

In imperial dynastic times Bei Di (Zhenwu) was a principal patron of soldiers and a protector of national security; in divine manifestations he leads his celestial forces to the aid of the terrestrial imperial forces. The heightened wave of superstition which took possession in northern China around 1900, known to foreigners as the Boxer Uprising, incited open fanaticism. People met secretly in temples and elsewhere under the sign of the mysterious and magical Zhenwu; spirit mediums spoke in his name, and young initiates fell to the ground in a trance before his image. All were assured of invulnerability from sword and bullet.

Traditional lore and legend about the Northern Emperor abound. Most Chinese will have heard of him probably at their grandmother's knee if, indeed, they have not read the novel about this hero, *Beiyou Ji* (Journey to the North), written *c.*1600 to complement *Xiyou Ji* (Journey to the West). The majority of people, however, would only be able to recount how he was appointed Guardian of the North by the Jade Emperor after fighting on the winning side during the legendary wars of the twelfth century BC. He defeated the Snake and Tortoise, the two magical allies of Mo Wang, the Demon King, and emerged the victor, barefooted and dishevelled.

A popular legend of the Northern Emperor was traditionally related over many successive nights by tea house storytellers. They would describe his imperial origins, how he was conceived by the wife of the emperor Qing Di, who dreamt that Laozi, the sage and founder of Daoism, came to her one night in a dragon carriage bearing a male baby from whom emanated brilliant rays of every colour. She soon found herself pregnant. Eighteen months later she gave birth to a son who was illuminated by a resplendent light. He succeeded to the throne when his father died but, realizing the instability of human existence, abdicated and retired to the hills where, after 800 incarnations, he became the first of many golden immortals.

During the period when the Northern Emperor was on earth as a human, destined to inherit a throne in heaven, people were primarily vegetarian. One of the many stories told about him relates how an evil man persuaded him to taste meat, which so revolted him that he cut open his stomach to wash both it and his intestines clean. During the process he was urgently summoned to heaven. One legend describes how his lungs (or stomach) and intestines turned into a snake and tortoise, both eventually following him to heaven. In time the two creatures, Snake and Tortoise, became humans and his civil and military aides; in temples, their images stand at floor level flanking Bei Di's altar.

Zhao Gongming

Zhao Gongming (Plate 7), also known as Xuantan Yuanshuai, Marshal of the Dark Altar, is General of the White Tiger.[4] Having captured and tamed a tiger during the mythical wars described in the *Fengshen Yanyi*, he made this beast his steed. He was then appointed in charge of gold, eventually becoming the popular wealth god, and, as president of the Celestial Ministry of Prosperity and Riches, he is responsible for a constant and regular source of income, but not for winnings.

Images of the Marshal of the Dark Altar are usually easy to identify, and his characteristics, taken in sum, are unique. He is either standing, sitting, or riding a tiger, which stands or sits beside him. In a few instances he is portrayed carrying a steel whip in one hand and a lump of gold, or a pearl, in the other. The latter can explode like a grenade when thrown at an enemy.

During the mythological wars described in the *Fengshen Yanyi*, Marshal Zhao Gongming used his magic to tame and ride a tiger, but he was best known for his pearl grenades. The evil King Zhou Xin of the Shang dynasty sent Marshal Zhao, with his tiger and knotted steel whip, to help attack and overcome Jiang Ziya. In the battle to break through Jiang's formations, Zhao inflicted a disastrous but not decisive defeat on Jiang and the Zhou forces. After the wars, Zhao was killed by magic; a combination of charms and an arrow fired at his effigy brought about his death. To avoid his spirit seeking revenge, Zhao Gongming was deified by the victors and honoured with the title Military God of Wealth.

Wang Lingguan

A number of Daoist deities, semi-demonic Spirit Officials or Lingguan, who are soldiers and bear military rank, are responsible for the protection of Daoist scriptures, and are at the same time deities of law and justice. The best known of these is Wang Lingguan, also known as General or Marshal Wang. He is the traditional protector of Daoist scriptures, whose image can be seen throughout China at the entrance to Daoist and many popular religion temples.

He is renowned among villagers as a potent destroyer of demons. Devotees quote Daoist folklore, repeating tea house storytellers' tales, mostly taken from the *Fengshen Yanyi*, which relate how he was deified as a reward for the assistance he gave to the victors during the mythic Shang–Zhou wars.

Wang was created the Heavenly Marshal of the Ministry of Fire, and is readily identifiable as a soldier, wearing 'tiger' armour—typical military armour with a tiger's-head stomacher—and the small Daoist crown. He usually has a reddish face, red beard, and three eyes. The two normal eyes are round and protrude slightly, but the third eye is vertical in the centre of his forehead. His mouth is partly open in anger, and he has 'ear-pressing tufts', two vertical, pointed tufts of hair aside the head that help to identify demons and semi-demonic beings. He holds a 'whip' (magic sword) above his head in his right hand, but his unique characteristic is the mystical sign he is making with his left hand: it is held forward at waist height, the middle finger extended, pointing vertically, with the other fingers and thumb entwined. This is the mystic sign of the Golden Light, a protection against demons and ghosts. He stands ready to obey any order from the Jade Emperor, to whom he is responsible.

Qing Long

Qing Long, the Blue Dragon, is a Daoist spirit and Commander of the East, one of the stellar deities of the Four Quadrants (Si Gong). His season is the spring, and he is a prominent symbol at weddings as the bridegroom's guardian. Qing Long's image in temples is rare, but when he appears he is paired with Bai Hu, the White Tiger; they stand at the entrance as guardians of the larger Daoist establishments. The Blue Dragon was identified in the *Fengshen Yanyi* as Deng Jiugong, the deified senior general of the evil Shang ruler. During the celestial battles described in the legends, Deng was wounded by Nazha, who had flung his magic bracelet and struck Deng in the arm, incapacitating him. He was then captured by General Ha, the Blower, and executed. Deified on the orders of Jiang Ziya, Deng was awarded the stellar realm of the Blue Dragon Star (Qinglong Xing).

Taibai Jinxing

Taibai Jinxing is a mythological Daoist immortal, the son of
Bai Di, the White Emperor, and his name means Evening
Star, or Venus. The *Fengshen Yanyi* refers to him as an aide
in the entourage of the Jade Emperor. Passing mention in
several storytellers' tales reveals little about him, though
one tale, a variant on the usual seduction story, claims that
heaven was scandalized when Taibai Jinxing, charmed by
two celestial weaving girls, was led off to a cave where he
remained with them, alone, for forty-six days. This escapade
was uncovered during a celestial inquiry into the cause of a
lengthy drought. Taibai Jinxing, responsible for rain, having
been discovered and escorted back to his post, quickly
brought rain to the parched region, and the weaving girls
saved their skins by retiring to remote celestial palaces.

Notes

1   When talking to devotees it is normally an affront to refer to him as
the Monkey God.

2   Geomancy (Chinese *fengshui*) concerns location, while astrology is
concerned with dates and times, auspicious or otherwise.

3   The Snake and Tortoise can be seen in Han-dynasty funerary
chambers opposite the White Tiger, the Vermilion Bird, and the Azure
Dragon. Bei Di, the Northern Emperor, is chief of the four spirits of the
Four Quadrants or Four Palaces, Si Gong, who in great antiquity ruled the
four quarters of the universe.

4   The White Tiger, however, is widely known as a dangerous spirit
and one to be avoided at all costs. Devotees usually propitiate Zhao
Gongming to protect themselves from the White Tiger.

3
The Creation of the Universe

THE CHINESE CREATION myth describes how a few supernatural spirits transformed the chaos of primordial times into the universe as we know it.

Hongjun Laozu

Hongjun Laozu (Fig. 3.1), one of the great Daoist masters, is the personification of the vital principle in nature before the creation of the world. He is the Great Ancestor, a mythical character referred to in the *Fengshen Yanyi* as Master of the Patriarchs, said to have trained not only the first Daoist patriarch, Laozi,[1] but also most of the earliest immortals and teachers. The *Fengshen Yanyi* also describes how Hongjun

3.1 Hongjun Laozu, a great Daoist Master, is the personification of the vital principle in nature before the creation of the world. Singapore.

Laozu mediated between the three conflicting heroes who were later deified as the San Qing Daozu (Three Pure Ones). Observing them in desperate battle, Hongjun was determined to bring about peace between them. He assembled them within Jiang Ziya's camp, all in one tent, where he made them kneel before him and where he lectured on the evils of helping the tyrant Zhou Xin, wicked king of the Shang dynasty. Hongjun Laozu then gave each a pill, which he required them to swallow without question. Having done so, Hongjun explained that the pills would instantly explode and kill any of them harbouring an evil thought.

San Qing Daozu

Most Daoists see creation as the work of a triad of gods, San Qing Daozu, the Three Pure Ones (Plate 8), whose images can be seen in a great many Daoist temples. They are the supreme deities of the Daoist pantheon who rule the entire cosmos from the highest heavens. In the *San Qing Jing* (Doctrine of the Three Pure Ones), the Three are the symbolic personification of the three life principles of breath (*qi*), vital essence (*jing*), and spirit (*shen*). The Three, said to live in separate heavens corresponding to the three original divisions of the cosmic ether, are:

Yuanshi Tianzun, the deity of the Beginning who represents primeval origins, and who formulated the heavens and earth. He is said to have dominated the first phase of the creation of the cosmos and is the Perfect One, the Jade Pure (Yu Qing), in charge of the Heaven of the Heavenly Ones.

Lingbao Tianzun, the Highest Holy One, the High Pure (Shang Qing), and the Heavenly Elder of the Spiritual Treasure. He represents energy and activity, is in charge of the Heaven of the Perfect Ones (Zhenren), and devised the interaction of yin and yang, as well as the doctrine for the heavens and earth. He dominated the second phase of the creation of the cosmos.

Shenbao Tianzun, the Greatest Holy One, the Supreme Pure (Tai Qing). He represents mankind, and was later incarnated as the philosopher Laozi. He is now in charge of the third and lowest heaven, that of the immortals. He dominated the third phase of the creation of the cosmos, and later inspired the formation and development of religious Daoism.

Yuanshi Tianzun, the Primordial Heavenly Lord, existed within the galactic void for millions of years without change, and is described by some as the First Cause, the primeval spirit without beginning and without end, the source of all truth. His doctrine leads to immortality. He was formed from the 'original breath' (*qi*) before the world began.

In the *Fengshen Yanyi* he is referred to as the senior Daoist deity who authorized the deification of the ministers and warriors after the struggle leading to the overthrow of the Shang dynasty. He taught all Daoist deities of the highest grades; however, his language was so abstruse that he had to use an interpreter, the mythic Old Immortal of the South Pole, Nanji Tianzun. A legend recorded in the *Fengshen Yanyi* describes how, despairing of the world and mankind, Yuanshi Tianzun resigned from the throne of the Supreme Deity and retired to the Kunlun Mountains in far western China. He was then succeeded by the Jade Emperor.

Conflicting myths are confusing and inconsistent about the succession of gods. Yuanshi Tianzun was one of the earliest distinguishable deities[2] to appear in Daoism, his name appearing in mystic songs in the fourth and third centuries BC, whereas the Jade Emperor was only revealed towards the end of the first millennium AD. On scrolls and in images, Yuanshi Tianzun is usually represented as a scantily dressed elderly man with a topknot and grey beard, sitting on a lotus.

The Three Ancient Emperors, San Guan Dadi (see Chapter 6), often confused with the Three Pure Ones, form another triad common in popular religion temples. The three are usually personified as the triad of the Jade Emperor as the Celestial Emperor, or Emperor of Heaven (Tian Huang); Pangu as the Emperor of the Earth (Di Huang); and Laozi as the Emperor of Mankind (Ren Huang).

Pangu

To some, the earliest deity was Yuanshi Tianzun, but to the majority of devotees Pangu (Fig. 3.2) is the principal contender for the honour of primacy. He was a moribund

3.2 Pangu chiselled out the universe, put order into chaos, and separated the earth from the heavens. He is the progenitor of mankind. Author's personal collection.

spirit who emerged from the vast mundane egg when all was darkness and confusion, and is the mythological culture hero who chiselled out the universe, put order into chaos, separated the earth from the heavens, and became the progenitor of mankind. Some legends limit his talent to starting creation, and although Pangu was first recorded in legend before the third century AD, oral tradition probably goes back a further thousand years.

Legend about Pangu's works maintains that to fashion the universe the giant Pangu slaved for 18,000 years, chiselling rocks as they drifted across the skies. He was helped only by a dragon, phoenix, unicorn, tiger, and tortoise, and died as the task was reaching its climax, with his body becoming the features of the earth. As he toiled so he grew and grew until, with a mighty thrust, he pushed up the heavens and pushed out space to encompass the whole of the universe. His head became the uplands, his breath the wind, his voice became thunder, and his eyes the sun and moon. His blood became rivers, his veins and muscles the rocks, and his flesh the soil, with his skin becoming the cultivated land. His sweat fell as rain, and his bones and teeth became the inorganic matter. The union of two puffs of his breath brought forth the first humans, a youth and a maiden, the descendants of whom in the fullness of time spread over the whole world.

Pangu's image usually represents him as dwarfish, primeval, and dark skinned. He is bare to the waist, dressed in a simple skirt and necklet of leaves, or an animal skin. He is bald with bumps, incipient 'horns', on his forehead; he is frequently portrayed carrying a mallet and chisel. In several temples in Malaysia and Java an image said to be that of his wife stands on a separate side altar.

Jiu Tian Xuannü

According to numerous myths, early major cataclysmic events, such as the great flood, occurred during the era before the Five Sage Rulers of the Legendary Age (see Chapter 4). One such myth describes how Jiu Tian Xuannü, the Dark Lady of the Ninth Heaven, saved mankind from being inundated. This mythical deity of both Daoism and popular religion was frequently referred to simply as the Dark Lady (Xuannü). As an ancient empress of Chinese prehistory, she was regarded as one of the original ancestors and worshipped as such by country folk. When she descended to earth as a human she became known as Nü Wa (Fig. 3.3), now a major goddess of marriage and fertility, the patron of matchmakers and, until 1949, worshipped throughout China.

Jiu Tian Xuannü appears to have been first recorded as a male, though not as a ruler, with a human head and the body

3.3 Nü Wa, a mythical deity of both Daoism and popular religion, and an empress of Chinese prehistory. She is one of China's ancient rulers, and now a major goddess of marriage and fertility. Her celestial title is Jiu Tian Xuannü, the Dark Lady of the Ninth Heaven. Chiahsien, Taiwan.

of a snake or snail. Then, during the Han dynasty (206 BC–AD 220), this portrayal and concept changed to female, with portraits of her as a woman connected with immortality, sex, and war.

According to the *Fengshen Yanyi* she was born in Shanxi province, the younger sister of Fu Xi, the first of the Five Sage Rulers of the Legendary Age. She required from mankind the sanctity of marriage, and after people had sacrificed to her, the winds and rains became propitious and calamities abated. By the Han dynasty, a well-developed myth connected her with halting the cause of the cataclysmic flood and thereby saving the world. The *Fengshen Yanyi* describes how the demon Gong Gong, in a fit of fury, beat his head against the mountain which supported the north-west section of heaven, causing it to collapse. During the subsequent continuous torrential rain, Nü Wa heard a petition from mankind requesting her to fill in the black hole that had appeared in heaven's floor, and through which the waters were pouring and storm winds roaring. The Dark Lady expeditiously melted down many thousands of stones and poured the molten liquid into the hole, thereby patching heaven's floor. Because the stones came from a number of areas, the patch—stretching right across the heavens—was multicoloured, and when the rains ceased a rainbow appeared. She is also described by some as the moulder of mankind out of primordial mud; the leaders were moulded individually with care, and the commoners in a production line.

In the story of the fall of the Shang dynasty, Nü Wa used magical means to bewitch and draw Zhou Xin, the wicked king, into unspeakable depravities. She was furious because Zhou Xin, having caught a glimpse of her, had written a lewd and blasphemous poem about her on the wall of her temple.

She sought revenge for this impious act by changing three demons into beautiful women who were commanded to beguile Zhou Xin to his destruction. His cruel excesses alienated his most loyal subjects and even his own family plotted to destroy him. In due course Zhou Xin died by his own hand and Nü Wa was avenged.

Mention in early texts of her views on sexual mores have led to the present-day conviction that she, so offended by the way people immorally lived together, became the patroness of matchmakers; those wishing for the success of a planned marriage also pray to her. This despite the belief that she married her brother, Fu Xi, to repopulate the earth after the great flood. She is responsible for the long-standing custom whereby people of the same clan name have been forbidden to marry. She is a master of magic; an episode in the *Fengshen Yanyi* describes how she mounted her pheasant and flew towards the capital to confront the tyrant Zhou Xin. As she neared the city she encountered two jets of red light, which pierced the clouds and prevented her from flying on. She knew instantly that Generals Heng and Ha were responsible.

Shan Shen
Shan Shen, the God of the Local Mountain, is an impersonal deity who, like the Spirit of the Well, the God of the Bridge, and others, is an Earth God. These mythical spirits of the local hill or mountain are only rarely identified with a historical person or mythical creature, being simply the nameless Spirit of the Mountain. As keeper and controller of the hills, each is responsible for its mineral and arboreal wealth. Peasants pray to the Spirit Official of the inorganic matter of the hills so that he might reveal to them the

treasures concealed within. Peasants and herbalists pray to Shan Shen to protect them against wild creatures before they venture on to the hillsides to gather firewood or medicinal herbs. The Spirits of the Mountain, Well, Bridge, and so on are nearly always represented by a dressed stone dedicated to and bearing a simple title, such as 'The Spirit of This Mountain'.

Taiyin Xingjun

Taiyin Xingjun (Fig. 3.4), the Lady of the Yin (Goddess of the Moon), together with the Lord of the Yang (God of the Sun), are among the impersonal gods and early mythical deities of nature and of climate. These two together control light and dark, and hot and cold weather, and act as the main protective deities of farmers and deep-sea fishermen. They were among the legion of spirits who inhabited the fears and imaginings

3.4 Taiyin Xingjun, the Lady of the Yin (Goddess of the Moon), pictured here, who together with the Lord of the Yang (God of the Sun) controls light and dark, and hot and cold weather. They shine on all equally and protect mankind from evil influences. Seremban, Malaysia.

of early folk, and although their images can be seen on altars in temples, neither was ever human. Both these stellar deities are impartial, shining on all equally; they protect mankind from evil influences.

Notes

1 In the older Wade–Giles system of transliterating Chinese, and its earlier romanization by missionaries in China before the turn of the twentieth century, he was known as Lao Tzu.

2 During the Shang dynasty the earliest supreme being, referred to as Shang Di, was consulted by diviners on behalf of the chiefs of society for good fortune and protection. Shang Di can be considered both a single entity, and as the composite of the ancestral spirits of the former rulers of the dynasty. Although in earlier times Shang Di was more of an abstract concept, he later became increasingly personalized.

4

Prehistory and the Legendary Rulers

EACH OF THE Five Sage Rulers of the Legendary Age, referred to variously as chiefs, kings, or emperors, is said to have reigned some 100 years, and though in essence they are names regarded as individuals, in reality they represent dynasties prior to *c*.2500 BC. This representative role of the legendary rulers highlights major aspects of the development of Chinese civilization and culture, when civilizing inventions and policies credited to them were made. All five—formerly and still worshipped in temples—were followed by a lengthy period of semi-legendary reigns, ending with the fall of the Shang during the twelfth century BC.[1]

The most popular and commonly quoted list of five, all believed to have lived during the third millennium BC, are Fu Xi, Shen Nong, Huang Di, Yao, and Shun. The first three of these deified rulers are legendary culture heroes who created and developed early Chinese civilization; Yao and Shun were semi-historical human rulers and are dealt with in Chapter 5.

Fu Xi

Fu Xi (Plate 9), a primeval ruler, popularly thought of as the founder of China, is credited with the establishment of kingly rule and the creation of different ranks within the state, marriage laws, and the computation of time by inventing a form of calendar using a knotted cord. The Eight Trigrams (*bagua*) are also attributed to him. These formed the basis of a system of fortune telling using trigrams, eight groups of triple lines, each group a combination of three broken or unbroken lines, arranged in ranks. The *bagua* system has governed the lives of a great many Chinese ever since. Fu Xi is the Patriarch of the Eight Trigrams and patron of fortune tellers and *fengshui* specialists, whose advice is sought for the best site for a grave, a new home, or a new business. He planned and established the basis for social order using clan or family names to ensure registration for taxation; taught people to hunt and fish (his invention of the fishing net came from watching spiders); instructed them how to smelt iron and herd livestock; invented musical instruments; and taught people how to cook food.

Images of Fu Xi, noted on altars in Daoist and popular religion temples, portray him as a primitive man dressed in skins or leaves. In early reliefs and paintings, however, he was portrayed as a snake, as is his sister/wife, Nü Wa, the two often entwined together. In other portraits he has been depicted with a dragon's body and a bovine head.

His mother is said to have trodden in the footprint of a giant, or seen a shooting star, and miraculously conceived; she carried him for twelve months before he was born, in Shaanxi province.[2] Some Chinese denounce the couple for their incestuous relationship, but this was done to continue the human race after mankind had been drowned in the great flood. Local myth even locates their escape from the flood at the summit of a mountain near Linfen in Shanxi province, where they were borne by a pair of lions. Legend claims that Fu Xi was buried in Henan province, the centre of his cult.

Shen Nong

Shen Nong (Plate 10) was an early deity listed as one of the Shang Di (High Gods) of the Han royal house. He is regarded as the First Farmer, the founder of Natural Medicine, and, as both a Daoist and popular religion deity, the God of

Husbandry, or Agriculture. He was worshipped in all parts of China and is probably the best known of the Chinese culture heroes. His myth embodies the folk memory of the change in primitive China from Mesolithic hunters to Neolithic agriculturists. As a sagacious primeval ruler, he has been credited with inventing many of China's farming implements, introducing mankind to ploughs made of wood and to the art of cultivation of the Five Grains (Wu Gu): hemp, millet, rice, wheat, and pulse. He also established the concept of markets to exchange produce, and is said to have invented pottery and the axe.

Legends describe how Shen Nong became the first to analyse the beneficial and harmful properties of herbs and to list their efficacy by testing hundreds of them on himself. He is said to have had a transparent stomach so that whatever he ate could be observed; he often nearly died from these tests, until finally one day he did, whereupon his body turned black. His treatise[3] on medicinal herbs is still used by Chinese herbalists and is their highest authority on drugs. In Shanxi province, the home of Shen Nong, where anecdotes about him and his life circulated widely as recently as 1949, as though he had died only a few decades before, herbal doctors there referred to their 'Shen Nong Treatment', much as in the West we might speak of Fleming or Pasteur. Shen Nong is revered throughout China as the patron of farmers, as well as of native herbalists.

The earliest carvings and prints portray Shen Nong either as a snake with a human head and arms, or as an ordinary human holding a large, wide two-pronged spade. Today, however, his image on altars usually portrays him as one of the 'primitives', sitting on a rock or seat, dressed only in leaves and grass either wound round his neck, waist, and calves, or as a bolero and skirt of leaves. Customarily, his image depicts him as black-skinned, reflecting his death from poison, and in South China he is frequently shown clutching an ear of wheat or a rice stalk. However, in his northern home province of Shanxi he was and still is portrayed clutching a head of millet or sorghum.

Huang Di

Huang Di, the Yellow Emperor, is considered by the Han Chinese to be their direct forebear; many also believe him (rather than Fu Xi) to be the founder of China who lived in the heartland of the Yellow River Basin and who extended the frontiers in the east to the sea, in the north and west to the deserts and mountains, and in the south beyond the Yangzi River. Legend claims that when Shen Nong died a rebellion broke out in the south. Huang Di, the successor to Shen Nong, quelled this uprising and incorporated the southern regions into the Chinese empire. He developed civilized society as we now know it, aided by ministers of considerable genius, and is the most famous culture hero of Chinese mythology. To give a perspective to Chinese history, one can occasionally encounter in Chinese books a reference to a date, say AD 1911, the first year of the Republic, but also the 4,609th year of the Yellow Emperor.

Many orthodox Daoists regard him as the First Master, the first human to ascend to transcendency, and many devotees of popular religion hold him to be the ancestor of all the Chinese. It is not surprising, therefore, that the genealogies of a great number of Chinese clans claim the Yellow Emperor to be their patriarch.

During his long reign he cleared the brush, burned the forests, drained the marshes, drove out the wild animals, and made animal husbandry possible. Huang Di is variously said to have founded Daoism (some thousand years before Laozi), or to have studied it under an old sage, one of the many earlier incarnations of Laozi; domesticated cattle and horses; invented the wheeled vehicle, pottery, pestles and mortars, dyeing (imitating the colours of nature), bows and arrows, and armoured boats; instituted copper coins; developed yoga as a form of physico-religious alchemy, having himself received instruction from three female immortals, and acupuncture as a curative. He taught people to build houses, to make bricks and utensils, and metalwork; and is credited with instructing people on their duties to their ancestors and with fixing the sexagenary calendar cycle, which remained in use until 1911. He originated the fashioning of clothes and is the patron of tailors. Whereas Fu Xi and Shen Nong were primitive, prehuman beings, usually portrayed on altars wearing necklets and skirts of leaves, the Yellow Emperor, being semi-human and having introduced textiles to China, is depicted wearing clothes.

As with many legendary inventors and culture heroes, he would not have been a single person but rather a dynasty, the personification of folk memory of proto-Chinese emerging from Neolithic society. His existence in misty legend has been made that much more 'genuine' by the folk memory of his burial place in Huangling, a small town beside a Yellow River tributary in Shaanxi, halfway between Xian and Yanan, where his shrine stands amidst a few trees surrounded by yellow earth. In legend he achieved immortality and ascended to heaven on the back of a dragon in broad daylight, together with all his ministers and seventy of his ladies. The Yellow Emperor was fortunate in having a supportive queen. This was his primary wife, Leizu, also known as Yuan Fei, the daughter of a feudal chief. She was an extremely ugly woman but, in the immortal words of the

Yellow Emperor, 'She has all the womanly virtues, which are much more important.' Having introduced sericulture to China, teaching the Chinese how to rear silkworms, and how to spin and weave the silk, she became the patron of silkworm cultivators and weavers.

Cang Jie

Among the talented ministers who aided the Yellow Emperor, some are still today revered on Chinese altars. These include the legendary inventor of Chinese characters and writing, Cang Jie (Plate 11), who realized the need to record thought. He was also the president of a commission of learned men set up by the Yellow Emperor in about 2600 BC to continue and complete the labours of Shen Nong on natural history and the medical properties of plants. Once the skills of writing had been achieved, so the story goes, wild and evil people were less keen on being seen, as their evil deeds could now be recorded and passed on to the Courts of the Underworld. Cang was selected for his post as president because he had a face like a dragon, with a large mouth and bright eyes. His tomb was situated in Shandong province. Sketches and images of Cang Jie show a barefooted, bearded middle-aged man with shoulder-length hair, dressed in robes of leaves with a leaf necklet. Most startling of all, he is portrayed as having four eyes, one pair immediately above the other.

Cang is the patron of public storytellers in central China, and of engravers and those in the paper-making and book businesses in northern China, as well as the patron of young scholars. A side hall dedicated to Shen Nong in Macau's old Guan Yin temple contains an image of Cang Jie towering over a row of small benches and desks, a school classroom.

In years gone by the incinerator in Cang Jie temples or halls was the place to burn all waste paper bearing characters, out of respect for the written word. Such scraps of paper were carefully recovered, often off the street by beggars employed by the literati.

Chi You

Chi You (Plate 12), the first great rebel, is regarded by early chroniclers as the man who destroyed the peace and innocence of primitive society.[4] He headed a confederacy of Eighty-one Brothers with the bodies of beasts, but with human speech and foreheads of iron, who fed on the dust of the earth. Reputed to have been the inventor of weapons, he raised the standard of rebellion against the ruling king and tried to dethrone him, but was defeated in battle after escaping in a mist that he had created by magic. He was pursued by a loyal general who, using a wooden figure on his chariot with an outstretched arm always pointing south, was able to find his way through the mist and kill Chi You. The loyal general, consenting to ascend the throne after this victory, took the title of Huang Di, the Yellow Emperor.

An extraordinary image of Chi You stands on a crowded altar table before the main altar in a back street temple in Tainan, southern Taiwan. The temple keeper knew that Chi You was a renowned rebel, but he had no idea why the image had been carved and placed on his altar as a donation by a local devotee. The image, difficult to describe, portrays a primitive creature standing on its rear legs. Chi You holds what looks like a small triangular flag in his hands. His arms appear to be scaly and he has no clothes as such; the head is a revolting, bulging mass of flesh with the ears of a cat and a very large mouth.

Zhu Rong

Zhu Rong, one of a number of legendary heroes on the board of the Celestial Ministry of Fire, is a repulsive, fierce, red-haired demonic figure. He was first mentioned in the Han-dynasty *Li Ji* (Book of Rites), one of the Confucian classics that lays down the rules of conduct for government and family; he was probably the legendary discoverer of fire, popularly changed into a deity and said to mete out punishment by setting people's houses alight. He lived during the time of the Yellow Emperor and became his successor on the imperial throne. Many folk tales involve Zhu Rong; possibly the best known involves his wish, when still a very young man, to achieve immortality. Shou Xing, the God of Longevity, told him that he would have to wait until he had become emperor and only then, after his death, when buried on the slopes of Heng Shan, the Sacred Mountain of the South in Hunan province, would he achieve immortality. The temple on the peak of Heng Shan contains an image of Zhu Rong to this day, where he is revered as the God of Fire.

Notes

1   It is usual when writing about Chinese mythical deities to draw a clear line of division between myth and legend. This has not always been possible, as tales told about the Five Sage Rulers of the Legendary Age have included significant elements of mythology as well as legend; it must also be borne in mind that the main focus here is on the mythical gods, and not on the mythical beings described in Chinese fables.

2   Francis H. Nichols, in his *Through Hidden Shensi* (London: Newnes, 1902), noted that about an hour after leaving Xian he passed a little temple that was in no way different from thousands of other little places of worship in Shaanxi. An inscription said, 'On this spot the Great Fu Xi was born.'

3   *Shen Nong Bencao Jing* (Shen Nong Pharmacopoeia).

4   Chi You was the chieftain of a tribal alliance formed by several nationalities in southern China about 5,000 years ago. The Miao (Hmong) of China consider him their prime ancestor.

1. Jiang Ziya, chief minister of the spirit world, and commander-in-chief of all celestial armies. He awarded posts and titles to the heroes and worthies at the canonization ceremony, when a great number of deities were created to rule over the destinies of mankind. Qishan, Shaanxi.

2. Jiang Ziya in the presence of the evil king, Zhou Xin, and his demonic concubine, Da Ji. Temple mural illustrating scenes from *Fengshen Yanyi*, Shaanxi province.

3. King Zhou Xin, the tyrannical last ruler of the Shang dynasty, died within his palace, engulfed in a fire started on his orders after he realized the war was lost. Temple mural illustrating scenes from *Fengshen Yanyi*, Shaanxi province.

4. Er Lang, a legendary hero who helped Jiang Ziya overthrow the Shang dynasty. A benevolent deity who helps those in need, he drives away demons, wards off demonic influences, and is the patron of dogs. Chia I, Taiwan.

5. Nazha San Taizi, the Third Prince, also known as Li Nazha, is an exorcising spirit famous for his exploits, a powerful deity despatched by the Jade Emperor to subdue the demons raging through the world. Putuo Shan, Zhejiang.

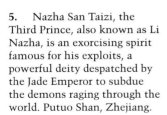

6. Tai Sui, president of the Celestial Ministry of Time, and Ruler of the Year, is an arbiter of the destiny of mankind, and God of the Sexagenary Cycle. All sixty images of Tai Sui, one for each year of the cycle, are represented at this major temple. Nanchang, Jiangxi.

7. Zhao Gongming, Marshal of the Dark Altar, is also General of the White Tiger. He is a popular God of Wealth, responsible for a constant and regular source of income, but not for winnings. Cholon, Vietnam.

8. San Qing Daozu, the Three Pure Ones, the supreme trinity of Daoism and the supreme deities of the Daoist pantheon. Yuanshi Tianzun (centre), Lingbao Tianzun (left), and Shenbao Tianzun (right), Kowloon, Hong Kong.

9. Fu Xi, the first of the legendary rulers, is claimed to be the founder of China. He is known as the Patriarch of the Eight Trigrams, portrayed here holding an eight-trigram disc. Lao Shan, Shandong.

10. Shen Nong, regarded as the First Farmer and the founder of natural medicine, is the God of Husbandry, or Agriculture. His myth is the folk memory of the transition in primitive China from Mesolithic hunters to Neolithic agriculturists. Lao Shan, Shandong.

11. Cang Jie, one of the Yellow Emperor's talented ministers, was the legendary inventor of Chinese characters and writing. Usually portrayed with four eyes, one pair immediately above the other, here he is shown with three pairs of eyes. Tungkang, Taiwan.

12. Chi You, here depicted as a primitive creature, was the first great rebel, regarded by early writers as the man who destroyed the peace and innocence of primitive society. He oppressed the people until destroyed by the Yellow Emperor. Tainan, Taiwan.

13. Yao, the Lord of the Golden Age and first of the Three Sage Kings, flanked by his most able ministers; on the left, the minister responsible for the invention of writing and divination; on the right, the minister responsible for formalizing agriculture. Yaocheng, near Taigu, Shanxi.

14. Shun, second of the Three Sage Kings, instituted penal laws, divided the kingdom into provinces, and deepened the rivers. Portrayed here on the main altar of the Chen clan temple. Kuala Lumpur, Malaysia.

帝大官三宮上玉

15. San Guan Dadi, the Three Great Primordial Rulers, and the Lords (or Controllers) of Heaven, Earth, and the Waters, were sent down by the Jade Emperor to govern the earth. Tian Guan (centre), the Ruler of Heaven, is occasionally identified as the Jade Emperor. Di Guan (left) is the Ruler of Earth, and Shui Guan (right) is the Ruler of the Waters. Taipei, Taiwan.

16. Xi Wangmu, Queen Mother of the West, and most senior goddess in the Daoist celestial hierarchy, dwells in the Western Heavens where she is surrounded by legions of immortals. Old mural in a village temple south of Taiyuan, Shanxi. (Photograph courtesy of Jennifer Welch.)

17. Yuexia Laoren, the Old Man of the Moon, is the divine matchmaker. He joins intended couples even before they are born, binding them with an invisible red thread which, once knotted, links them absolutely. Western Hills, Beijing.

18. Bixia Yuanjun, Princess (or Goddess) of the Azure Clouds, a daughter of Dongyue Dadi, Lord of the Underworld. She is a protectress of women and children, and patron of wet nurses. Western Hills, Beijing.

19. Houtu, the Spirit of the Earth, is an early Chinese deity, an earth mother regarded as a goddess of agrarian fecundity. This image sits on the main altar in the Houtu cult centre, Wanrong county, southern Shanxi.

20. Lei Gong, the Thunder God, is an early nature deity who averts evil. Not permitted to punish on his own authority, he smites wrongdoers only after receiving direct instructions from the Jade Emperor. Kaifeng, Henan.

21. Feng Bo (Feng Shen), the Wind Earl, is a minor mythological deity of the elements. He is paired with Yu Shi, the Master of Rain, and stands on altars together with Lei Gong, the Thunder God, and Dian Mu, the Lightning Matron. Taiyuan, Shanxi.

22. Yu Shi, the Master of Rain, and Feng Bo, the Wind Earl, both nature deities. Yu Shi has the head of a dragon and carries the twig with which he sprinkles rain from his bowl onto the earth below. Here Feng Bo has the very unusual attribute of eyes out on stalks. Jade Emperor Temple, Kepala Betas near Butterworth, Malaysia.

23. Long Wang, the Dragon Kings, live in palaces at the bottom of their oceans, rivers, and lakes. They are the guardians of the watery world, and the moving spirits of storms and rain. Taiyuan, Shanxi.

24. Hei Di Tianwang, the Heavenly Lord, the Black Emperor, is a local cult deity only seen in a rural village temple on the Guangxi– Hunan border. He has protected the village from evil ever since the villagers built a temple in his honour.

5
The Three Sage Kings

THE REIGNS OF three semi-mythical rulers of feudal China, Yao, Shun, and Yu, marked the dawn of historical China. They are commonly known as the Sage Kings and regarded as perfect men; they were chosen, or elected, and not successive blood-descendants. Yao and Shun, the last two of the Five Sage Rulers of the Legendary Age (see Chapter 4), are also two of the most conspicuous names in Chinese history, ideal rulers against whom every sovereign has been measured since their day. The Chinese have endowed them with every conceivable virtue, and acknowledge them as the first and most sagacious of Chinese rulers. Though partly legendary, they are strongly believed to have lived, if not as individuals, then each as a line of major chieftains during the third and second millennia BC. Their fame originates from Confucius's reference to Yao as 'great indeed', Shun as 'entirely good', and Yu as 'without deficiencies'. Historically, it has long been accepted that Yu was the 'progenitor of the Xia dynasty' (c.2205 BC), even if some consider him mythical, whereas Yao and Shun are regarded as dynasties and culture heroes.

Yao
Yao (Plate 13), the Lord of the Golden Age, is said to have reigned for 98 years from 2357 BC, after which he abdicated in favour of Shun. He was a man of many parts and a soldier of renown; he pacified the south, and also expanded his kingdom to the north and west. Yao introduced orderly government and civilization to China, performing the functions of both ruler and high priest. In legend he was a

master of divination and read the future by interpreting the cracks on ox bones and tortoise shells caused by the application of hot irons. Many claim that he established a legal system that united justice with compassion, consistency, and great discernment. He selected capable men to aid his government and with their help he observed the heavenly bodies, not as an astronomer, but simply to assist farmers in knowing the right times to sow and harvest crops.

As with all legendary figures, Yao's features were exaggerated and descriptions embroidered upon down the centuries. After a miraculous birth, he was noted to have eyebrows in eight colours, and nine orifices in his body instead of the normal seven.

His tomb and temple at Linfen in Shanxi were described a century ago as active centres of worship, with the temple built, so it was claimed, on the site where Yao kept his residence before his enthronement. It is still regarded as the cult centre, though the temple is now a museum, not a working temple. His image on the main 'altar' (of the museum), in the bright, solid colours used in northern China, depicts him as an awesome ruler sitting on a throne.

Yao had nine sons. He considered them all incompetent to take over the throne, so as a successor he selected a Henan native, also named Yao, but known as Shun, who, in spite of humble birth, was renowned for being virtuous, exceptionally filial, and the source of every good action of justice and humanity. Shun did not disappoint Yao. Yao gave him two of his daughters as wives and tested him with an official post to judge his ability to rule. Finally at ease, Yao abdicated in Shun's favour.

Legend states that Yao found his successor 'with Heaven's assistance' when he encountered a peasant, Shun himself, ploughing with two oxen. The farmer held a dustpan (basket) instead of a whip, and explained that rather than strike the oxen to greater efforts he beat on the pan, which sounded to the other ox as though his partner was being beaten, and thus each made greater efforts.

Shun

All tales agree that Shun (Plate 14) rose to prominence by sheer ability. He instituted various penal laws, divided the kingdom into provinces, and deepened the rivers. He had the face of a dragon, a big mouth, was very tall, and black in colour. He is said to have invented the writing brush and to have had four eyes (or double pupils in his two eyes), though images of him do not portray him as such.

His father was widowed early and married a second wife by whom he had another son. The father and stepmother developed a great dislike for Shun and tried to kill him several times. Despite this, Shun continued to exhibit such exemplary conduct towards his father and stepmother that he eventually won them over; ever since he has been included in the twenty-four examples of filial piety.

Shun was made a magistrate and promoted to governor only three years later. A different tale has him serving Yao for twenty-eight years, draining and clearing the land, growing the Five Grains, and driving off wild animals, before he was proclaimed ruler on the death of Yao.

Shun, like Yao before him, lived simply and was the earliest of China's rulers to make the long, arduous pilgrimage up rugged Tai Shan, the sacred mountain in Shandong province, to offer up sacrifices on its summit. He is said to have died at the age of 100 during an inspection tour of the southern provinces. Others believe that he died on an expedition against aboriginal tribes south of the Yangzi, and was buried at Jiuyi Shan in Hunan, where a temple in his honour stood for many centuries. A local legend in Hunan relates how, when Shun died, his body was lost in a flood and his two consorts searched the banks of the Xiang River, seeking the corpse and weeping inconsolably. Their tears stained the surface of the bamboo, which explains the origin of the famous spotted bamboo so beloved of poets.

Yu

Shun ruled for thirty-nine years before he too passed over his two sons, appointing as his successor one of his ministers. This talented engineer, named Yu (Fig. 5.1), was ordered to

5.1 Yu, third of the Three Sage Kings, and a talented engineer, is said to have tamed the untameable Yellow River, in Henan province, and built the canals around the city of Shaoxing, in Zhejiang province, where this image stands in a temple dedicated to him. Shaoxing, Zhejiang.

superintend the making of canals and embankments to remedy the ever-present menace of the Yellow River breaking its banks. He succeeded in controlling the major inundations and ravages of the mighty river, and the memory of these vast undertakings has remained engraved on Chinese minds. They still regard Yu with undying gratitude as the hero who tamed the untameable Yellow River.

Before the time of Shun, who was the last to follow the tradition, each succeeding ruler had been chosen for his wisdom, not his parentage. However, Yu, the last of these rulers by popular acclaim, was succeeded by his son, the founder and first emperor of a dynasty, the Xia, which lasted over 400 years. The practice of hereditary rule continued through all succeeding dynasties until the fall of the Qing dynasty in 1911.

Yu was reported to have three apertures in each ear, though more popular myths claim that he had the body of a snake with a human face, a tiger's nose, and the head of an ox. Legends claim that he was, variously, a descendant of the Yellow Emperor, or the result of a miraculous birth into a family of commoners; his mother was a virgin, his conception supernatural.

The best known tale describes how Yu, when one of Shun's ministers, was so devoted to the task of controlling the flood waters and rivers that he passed his home three times during his travels without once calling in. This even though he left home just four days after his marriage, and on one occasion he even heard the cries of his son whom he had never seen.

Images of the Great Yu have been recorded on a number of temple altars in northern, central, and eastern China, predominantly in Jiangsu, Zhejiang, and Sichuan provinces. His cult centre is the temple dedicated to him outside the East Gate of Kaifeng in Henan province.

The canals around the city of Shaoxing, not far from Hangzhou, are said to be one of his achievements, and his tomb, claimed by locals to be his cult centre, is located in the countryside just beyond the city.

Yao and Shun had their capital in Pingyang (today's Linfen), in Shanxi province, on the Fen River. Upon returning from his final pilgrimage, Yu ordered sacrifices to his ancestors in a temple that he founded three miles south of Pingyang; much later a temple was built there, dedicated to Yao and Shun, in which statues of the two deities stood some 60 feet high. The temple, now long gone, consisted of four courtyards enclosed within a mud wall. The Eastern Court was sacred to the Great Yu, third of the Three Sage Kings. Next to it, the Chief Court was sacred to Yao, and the Western Court to Shun. Today a large temple dedicated solely to Yao in Linfen municipality contains a large image of the king; both temple and image have been rebuilt since their destruction in the Cultural Revolution (1966–76).

6

Mythical Deities of Popular Legend

THE DEVELOPMENT OF belief in a supreme deity in China is far from clear. In earliest times, the all-seeing, all-powerful, unseen god was known as Shang Di, the Supreme Emperor or All Highest.[1] Even the late Chairman Mao used the term Shang Di, when he stated that he 'was seventy-two and soon going to see God'. This unseen Heavenly Lord was increasingly personified and gradually divorced from the abstract concept in the official ceremonies. By the Tang dynasty (618–907) he had become the common man's Jade Emperor, Yu Huang Dadi, regarded as the Supreme Lord of the Universe, and the celestial equivalent of the terrestrial emperor of China.

The Jade Emperor

In 1012, according to a popular legend, the Song Emperor Zhen Cong announced with great pomp that he had been visited in a dream by an immortal with a letter from the Jade Emperor, Yu Huang Dadi. This announcement was made to divert his ministers from an unfortunate treaty he had been obliged to sign with barbarian tribes. In the letter the Jade Emperor explained that the Song emperor was an incarnate descendant of himself, the Jade Emperor. Shortly after this Zhen Cong issued an edict proclaiming that whenever the Jade Emperor appeared in a dream, he had always identified himself as the Master of Heaven and Earth, and the Incarnation of the Dao. This state recognition by the Emperor Zhen Cong made the Jade Emperor the most important deity in the pantheon.

Although the Jade Emperor only became prominent during the last thousand years, he is the mythological deity revered all over China as the Supreme Ruler of the Heavens and the Underworld, and Protector of Mankind. To the man-in-the-street, all Buddhist, Daoist, and popular religion deities are subordinate to the Jade Emperor, and well-timed worship of the Jade Emperor can secure a writ of pardon for a soul in the Underworld. While he is concerned with running the bureaucracy of the celestial world, meting out justice and help, he delegates day-to-day responsibilities to his celestial ministers and judges.

A supreme sovereign of the universe is not to be approached lightly, nor is he approached directly, usually receiving devotional offerings and only very rarely pleas, principally through intermediaries. He is also believed to have the final say over natural conditions; in northern China particularly, people prayed to the Jade Emperor for protection from natural disasters and for conditions leading to a good harvest. Some prayed to him for remission of sins and fulfilment of desires, and in places, at a special ritual, he was invoked for male offspring. In many parts of China the Jade Emperor was considered too holy, too awesome, and too powerful to be represented by an image, and only a tablet bearing his title was permitted on altars.

Despite being all-powerful and commanding an enormous pantheon, in mythology the Jade Emperor is frequently duped and outwitted, as indeed the Chinese well know their terrestrial emperors were treated. This does not mean that he was not feared—his forces include powerful spirit armies capable of destroying anyone or anything that offends him.

Despite being an awesome, all-powerful deity, he was an upstart and an opportunist, a mere commoner who claimed the post when it was awarded at the end of the Shang–Zhou wars. All vacancies for the posts of minister and senior official had been filled, leaving only that of the Jade Emperor, which Jiang Ziya was reserving for himself. When offered the post, Jiang Ziya paused with customary courtesy and asked the people to 'wait a second' (*deng-lai*) while he considered. However, having called out *deng-lai*, an opportunist, Zhang Denglai, hearing his name, stepped forward, prostrated himself, and thanked Jiang for creating him the Jade Emperor. Jiang, stupefied, was unable to retract his words; he was, however, quietly able to curse Zhang Denglai, saying 'Your sons will become thieves and your daughters prostitutes.' Though this was not the ultimate fate of his daughters, many ribald stories are told about them.

Zao Jun

Between the twelfth day of the final lunar month and Lunar New Year's Day, the Jade Emperor personally receives the annual report on every household from each individual Kitchen God (see Chapter 8). This God of the Family Hearth (or Family Stove), known in Chinese as Zao Jun, is usually called the Kitchen God by foreigners. He is the most widespread of the deities found in Chinese homes, though he has nothing to do with either food or cooking. Rather, Zao Jun is the family tutelary deity in charge of the family's destiny, and is a Celestial Inspector, the domestic representative of the Jade Emperor who oversees and reports on the behaviour of the family.

From these reports the Jade Emperor examines everybody's conduct and adds his comments to the dossier kept on every living person against the day of death, when each human is summoned to enter the Courts of the Underworld for judgement.

Qi Xiannü

The popular legend of the Weaving Girl and the Cowherd describes how the Seventh Maid, Qi Xiannü, the seventh daughter of the Jade Emperor, was very lonely and so fled to Earth where she married a lowly but handsome cowherd. Her father was furious and ordered her to return. When she refused to leave her husband the two were separated by the Jade Emperor and banished to separate stars in the universe. The cowherd continued to seek her and wandered across the heavens; however, after a passionate plea from his daughter, the Jade Emperor eventually permitted them to meet once a year, on the lunar 'double seventh' (seventh day of the seventh month), when they cross a bridge of magpies over the Milky Way.

Originally, the Seventh Maid was prayed to not only for a good husband but also for help in weaving, and in most areas she was the patron deity of cloth weavers and seamstresses. This is one of the few popular romantic stories and the nearest the Chinese get to a Goddess of Love. Young girls have celebrated her festival annually by showing their skill at embroidery, one of the manifestations of their charm, to a prospective husband.

In another version of the tale, she is the seventh daughter of the Kitchen God, responsible for weaving cloth and sewing for the gods. Having married a cowherd, her absence irritated her customers as their darning and repairs were not being done. The gods demanded her recall to heaven to continue her labours, but allowed her to meet her husband one day each year.

San Guan Dadi

A trinity of deities of mythical origin, known as the San Guan Dadi (Plate 15), is the source of all happiness and forgiveness of sins. They are the Three Ancient Emperors, or more properly, the Three Great Primordial Rulers, and the Lords (or Controllers) of Heaven, Earth, and the Waters, popular for their ability to avert calamities and sickness. The trinity represents the mystic side of Daoism, and was associated with monasteries rather than temples of popular religion. The Jade Emperor sent the trinity down to govern the earth, and to observe the thoughts and deeds of all people.

The trinity, all of whom are stellar deities, with joint and individual responsibilities, is comprised of: **Tian Guan**, Ruler of Heaven, outranked only by the Jade Emperor with whom he is often identified, who bestows happiness, freedom, and prosperity; **Di Guan**, Ruler of Earth, often identified with Shen Nong (God of Agriculture), or Pangu (Creator of the Universe), judge of the sins of mankind, who grants remission to those who mend their ways; and **Shui Guan** (known in some places as Ren Guan), Ruler of the Waters, often identified with Laozi, controller of floods and dispeller of evils and pestilence, who frees people from adversity, sickness, and an unhappy destiny. The three are also known by their imperial titles: Tian Huang, Emperor of Heaven; Di Huang, Emperor of the Earth; and Ren Huang, Emperor of Mankind.

Xi Wangmu
The Western Heavens are the Mountains of the Immortals, the Kunlun, located far to the west of China, a land where heaven and earth meet and where the sun sets. Chinese myths describe the Kunlun as the home of Xi Wangmu, Queen Mother of the West (Plate 16), where, surrounded by legions of immortals, she resides in her garden of peaches beside the Jade Green Lake. The Queen Mother of the West

is a Daoist and popular religion goddess, the ruler of the Western Heavens, and the Controller of Time and Space, and of death. She is the most senior goddess in the Daoist celestial hierarchy, and by the Tang dynasty she had also become a leading popular religion deity.

Xi Wangmu is one of China's most ancient cult figures. She (or a deity with similar title) is mentioned in Shang-dynasty oracle bone inscriptions, and by the first century AD she had evolved into an extremely popular deity, revered at home and in temples, whose likeness appeared in numerous Han-dynasty works of art. In prehistory, though, she was a monster, an ugly mountain-tiger spirit with a tail and sharp teeth, and during the Han dynasty she was also described as a frightening being, an unkempt long-haired goddess in human form, with the teeth of a tiger, and the tail of a leopard. This image of her gradually changed; by the tenth century AD she had become a cultured and attractive female immortal (Fig. 6.1), transformed finally into the dowager goddess, even though she had never actually lived as a human being, and has no personal name. She is a deity formed of fundamental essence, of a Prior Heaven (Xiantian), from before the creation.

In her various incarnations, Xi Wangmu has been the mother of the Jade Emperor, Confucius, Laozi, and Sakyamuni Buddha. Some claim that she is married to the Jade Emperor, by whom she had nine sons and twenty-four daughters, all of them immortals. Most believers, however, claim that she is married to a quaint old man, Dongwang Mugong, the Royal Count of the East, whose image is rarely depicted on altars.

As Queen of the Immortals, Xi Wangmu presides over conventions of the most important immortals conducting philosophical discussions, and has each of the tens of

6.1 Xi Wangmu, Queen Mother of the West. Lao Shan, Shandong.

thousands of immortals reporting to her and paying obeisance prior to leaving the Western Heavens to take up posts in the human world. A popular story in Chinese literature describes how during preparations for her main banquet, held only once every three thousand years—when the peaches of immortality come into season—and to which all the immortals are invited, the Monkey King drank all the elixir of long life, and consumed all the peaches of immortality before anyone could stop him.

Chang E

The Goddess of the Moon, Chang E, or Heng E[2] as she was first called, is a mythical goddess of great beauty who dwells in the Palace of the Immortals on the moon. She is the daughter of the God of the Yellow River (He Bo), and a special patron of women, prayed to by wives who need solace or protection from evil husbands. The legend of Chang E begins with her husband, Hou Yi the renowned archer, who had been rewarded with the potion of immortality by Xi Wangmu for shooting down nine of the ten suns that had been scorching the earth, causing drought and famine. The lone remaining sun now shines down with just the right amount of light and heat, thanks to Hou Yi. However, Chang E purloined and swallowed the elixir, thus becoming an immortal, but then had to flee the wrath of her husband. She fled to the moon, where she is now stranded, accompanied only by a hare and unable to return to earth (Fig. 6.2). The

6.2 Chang E, the Goddess of the Moon, with her hare who busily grinds an elixir of longevity. Guan Yin Temple, Jalan Burma, Penang, Malaysia. (Photograph courtesy of Jennifer Welch.)

hare is said to be visible on clear nights on the face of the moon, endlessly pounding the elixir of immortality with his pestle and mortar. Poor Chang E is now immortal but at the price of being unutterably lonely and cold.

Yuexia Laoren

Another figure associated with the moon is Yuexia Laoren (Plate 17), the Old Man of the Moon, who is also the divine matchmaker. Many Chinese believe he binds together intended couples even before they are born, tying them with an invisible red thread which, once knotted, links them forever, despite human wishes and machinations to the contrary. The Chinese have a saying that marriages are made on the moon.

Shou Xing

Shou Xing, the Stellar God of Longevity, known also as Shou Laoren, or the Old Immortal of the South Pole (Nanji Tianzun), is one of the San Xing, Three Stellar Gods (Fu, Lu, Shou), three old men representing the most desirable blessings: good fortune; happiness, which includes having sons and grandsons; prosperity; and longevity. Shou Xing is a domestic rather than a public deity, prayed to by individuals for long life, particularly by the 'elderly' on their fiftieth, sixtieth, and seventieth birthdays. His image is popularly regarded by many as a decorative object rather than a deity. One legend claims that Shou Xing was the old Patriarch Peng, who lived 'about a thousand years', spanning the mythical era of 2000–1000 BC; he married nineteen women and actually survived fifty-four of his sons. Shou Xing determines how long a human might live on earth. His unique image is easily recognizable as the venerable white-bearded old man with a broad smile, a domed and egg-shaped bald head said to be full of yang energy, very long ears hanging down to his shoulders, and a very high, furrowed forehead. He is depicted standing, in one hand carrying a gnarled staff on which is hung a magic fungus, and in the other a peach of longevity.

Bixia Yuanjun

Bixia Yuanjun, Princess (or Goddess) of the Azure Clouds (Plate 18), is a popular Daoist mythological deity, a protectress of women and children, and patron of wet nurses. She is often described as the Goddess of Maternity, and is usually surrounded by her assistants, a dozen maids holding, training, and breastfeeding babies and young children. Originally a very local, northern Chinese deity, her cult spread over the years. Centered on the sacred mountain in Shandong province, Tai Shan, where she became accepted as the daughter of Dongyue Dadi, Lord of the Underworld (see Chapter 8), her cult appears to have been developed by Daoists during the late Tang or early Song dynasties as a counterbalance to the growing influence of the Buddhist Goddess of Mercy, Guan Yin, who was rapidly becoming the most popular champion of women and children.

Notes

1   Missionaries introduced Christianity to China from the sixteenth century onwards. The Protestant missionaries elected to use the term Shang Di in reference to the God of their church, a convention followed to this day by the Protestants in China. Catholics, on the other hand, translated their version of God as Tian Zhu, the Lord of Heaven.

2   The name Heng E had to be changed to Chang E, as it was the personal name of the Tang Emperor Mu Cong, and was considered taboo to mention aloud. Chang E is not to be confused with Taiyin Xingjun, Lady of the Yin, who is another deity also known as Goddess of the Moon.

7

Daoist Deities of Nature, Agriculture, and Natural Phenomena

CHINA'S ECONOMY HAS always been based on agriculture, and it is therefore not surprising to see such a large proportion of temples in rural villages dedicated to the various gods of agriculture or to those who govern the forces of nature.

Houtu

Houtu, the Spirit of the Earth (Plate 19), is an early Chinese deity, part of the overall primitive belief in the Spirits of Land and Grain. Usually thought of as male, this deity has a bewildering number of manifestations, including that of an earth mother referred to as Houtu Furen; the image in the Houtu cult centre in Wanrong county of southern Shanxi portrays her as a matronly figure. As a goddess she was looked upon by many as the incarnation of ancient sages who developed agriculture, a goddess of agrarian fecundity.

During the Zhou dynasty, Houtu was referred to as the Spirit of the Earth, though it appears people first officially sacrificed to him in c.1100 BC. As the Spirit of the Earth he was believed to have charge over the Underworld, and as such was (and sometimes still is) revered and offered sacrifices after a death. In Malaysia, tablets bearing the two characters Hou and Tu stand beside several graves in a Chinese cemetery in Malacca, strengthening a suggestion that Houtu is the protector of grave sites. It is more likely, however, that as the Spirit of the Earth he demanded propitiation whenever the soil was disturbed, whether by farmers or by grave diggers. In Taiwan, temple custodians have suggested that Houtu, in his male form, is no more than the local earth god under a different title, and the protective deity of the neighbourhood.

Houtu as a patron deity of the soil has been confused with, or connected with, and possibly even replaced Sheji, the God of the Harvest, and Houji, the Lord of Millet, both shadowy deities of antiquity. It is often said that Houtu was an assistant to the Yellow Emperor, and Houji an assistant to Shun (last of the Five Sage Rulers of the Legendary Age and one of the Three Sage Kings). However, it could well be that Houtu, Sheji, and Houji are one and the same deity worshipped under different titles across China.

Sheji
Sheji, the God of the Harvest, perhaps better known as the God of Soil and Grain, is the focus of a nationwide agrarian cult and one of the oldest of the state cults, probably well established by the Zhou dynasty. Sheji is also one the earliest recorded agricultural deities worshipped by the emperors and their officials, but not by the common man. Large official altars dedicated to Sheji once stood west of the Imperial City in Beijing, and just outside the Palace City in Nanjing. Each was a single square stone altar on which five different coloured soils brought from various provinces were arranged. Tudi Gong (see Chapter 8), the tutelary Earth God whose images can be seen today in every village and in a number of houses, and who was first recorded during the Han dynasty (c.first century AD), has over the centuries largely displaced Sheji, though in some places Tudi has been identified with Sheji.

Scores of small shrines in rural areas in both Hong Kong and Macau are dedicated to Sheji, though few bear his title, or for that matter any title or inscription whatsoever. The inscription on a dressed stone in the hills above Saikung in Hong Kong's New Territories merely says 'Sheji, the Spirit who Protects the People'. Others at the edge of villages or bordering main footpaths bear similar simple inscriptions, his title or title and an honorific. Sheji is especially worshipped as a controller of insect pests. Farmers light three sticks of incense immediately before replanting seedlings, place them at the edge of their fields, and bow thrice to invoke the aid of both the Earth God and Sheji to secure a bountiful harvest. Like the local Earth God, Sheji is frequently told family news because he is responsible for the vicinity, and is concerned about people's problems. It is not uncommon to see a woman squatting before a Sheji shrine and talking aloud in a voice a pitch or two higher than normal, relating her news, and pausing every now and again to allow the deity to take it in.

Houji

According to legend, Houji, a descendant of the Yellow Emperor, was made Minister of Agriculture by Shun. Local legends vary, with some devotees claiming that he was the son of Shen Nong, second of the Five Sage Rulers of the Legendary Age; others that he was the primary ancestor of the Zhou dynasty who settled in northern Shaanxi province, and was later venerated as a divine hero and protector of crops. He is said to have given the people wheat and barley. He became the God of Fields and Crops, referred to in Western writings as the Lord of Millet and the God of Cereals.

Agricultural Deities

The main agricultural deities include Lei Gong, the Thunder God, and Feng Shen, the Wind God, who together with Yu

Shen, the Rain God, and Long Wang, the Dragon King (who regulates the waters), all control the atmospheric forces. Each of these gods has a divine obligation towards humans: the Rain God, for example, is responsible for adequate precipitation.

According to myth, the agricultural deities also have the ability to delay or overdo their responsibilities at whim, or as punishment for major human transgressions. This capacity validates the belief that such gods need to be propitiated either to stop disasters, or to prevent them from happening.

Terrifying floods and droughts have all too frequently devastated northern and central China, leading to destruction and mass starvation. This is reflected by the number of temples dedicated to the gods of the elemental forces. Famine, failure of rains, or unseasonable and massive floods were all attributed to the supernatural agency, and it was widely believed that there was a link between human behaviour and the actions of the deities. Torrential rain and floods were believed to be actively caused by the deities. Drought, on the other hand, was considered to be a non-event caused by inactivity on the part of the deities. The vagaries of some deities can be such that humans, suffering from these whims or punishments, and feeling free of guilt, can complain to the next higher-ranking deity about the unjustified treatment. If the complaint is found to be valid the deity concerned can be punished by his superior god by demotion or even, in some myths, by death. Other harmful natural phenomena were often believed to be due to the misconduct of terrestrial Chinese officials who had disrupted the cosmic harmony.

All major and most minor rivers in China have their own mythological or legendary deity, mostly euhemerized.

Lei Gong

The gods of natural phenomena are impersonal deities; this includes Lei Gong, the Thunder God (Plate 20), an early nature deity. This stern god is generally benevolent and works to avert evil. He was revered in the very early days because of the mystery and powers of nature that he controlled with his consort, Dian Mu, the Lightning Matron. Lei Gong and Lei Zhenzi, one of the Sons of Thunder whose image is identical with that of Lei Gong, are both awesome deities whose likenesses are carved into buildings to protect against lightning strikes. Lei Zhenzi, like Lei Gong, was born out of a celestial egg.

Lei Gong is a member of the five-deity Celestial Board of the Ministry of Thunder, subordinate to Lei Zu, with whom he is often confused. Lei Zu, President of the Board, is recognizable as a typical Daoist figure, a human dressed in gilded robes, holding a wish-fulfilling (ruyi) magic sceptre, with hair drawn up into a topknot, and a third eye in the centre of his forehead. After Lei Zu, the other members of the Board are: Lei Gong, the Thunder God, a bat-winged, bird-headed deity; Dian Mu, the Lightning Matron, with mirrors or, in rare cases, with lightning sparks in each hand; Feng Bo, the Wind Earl (Plate 21), with a flag and wind wheel; and Yu Shi, the Master of Rain (Plate 22), with the rain dragon or watering can.

Lei Gong is assisted by his consort in distinguishing between good and evil people, and in punishing the evil. The list within temples of the evil acts against which he takes action used to catalogue only capital crimes; nowadays it includes the filially impious, liars, and cheats, and threatens that he will impose physical discomforts on truants and lazy scholar-students. Children are told that Lei Gong will not harm them unless they tell lies. Good and virtuous people were never killed by thunder, only the unfilial, the adulterer, and those who waste good food. Lei Gong is also feared for being particularly merciless towards those who kidnap children, or who oppress widows and orphans. He causes damage to property and fields with his thunderbolts, while Dian Mu merely flashes her mirrors to cause lightning. Should someone be struck down by the noise of thunder—as opposed to lightning, which is generally disregarded by peasants—it is considered more than likely due to infidelity.[1] Such fatalities proved to the peasants the power of divine retribution. It is the sure punishment for philanderers, but can be a punishment for deeds committed in previous incarnations. Hence, a child struck down is assumed to have been guilty in one of his earlier lives. Although many fear Lei Gong's power, it is generally believed that he is a functionary, and not authorized to punish on his own authority: he punishes only after receiving instructions to do so directly from the Jade Emperor.

Long Wang

Daoist mythology spells out the organization of the Celestial Ministry of the Waters, in which the ministers, the numerous Long Wang (Dragon Kings) (Plate 23), live in their own palaces at the bottoms of their oceans, lakes, and rivers. They visit the heavens during the spring but return to the deep early every autumn. Dragon Kings are the guardian spirits of oceans, lakes, and rivers, but in some areas they are believed also to be the direct cause of earthquakes, fogs, and damage to river banks. They are also responsible for the rain clouds, and agricultural fertility resulting from adequate and controlled annual rainfall. As they are the moving spirits of storms and rain, Dragon Kings are also often blamed for floods and water catastrophes.

A Dragon King can only take orders from the Jade Emperor, and must under no circumstances take it upon himself to provide or withhold rain. Should a drought last too long, however, then images of the Dragon King or the City God are exposed to the sun's rays for days on end until he relents and provides rain.

One popular myth describes the punishment of a Dragon King for his disobedience. The Jade Emperor issued an order that rain was to fall heavily in the countryside and lightly in towns. That same day the particular Dragon King, in his human form, called on Gui Guzi, a famous fortune teller, who recognized the Dragon King despite his human disguise. Gui Guzi told him that he, the Dragon King, had received orders to make rain fall heavily in the countryside. To disprove Gui Guzi, and to show that he had misidentified him as the Dragon King, he switched the order, making it rain heavily in towns and lightly in the countryside. Several people were drowned in the cities and the Jade Emperor, furious, sentenced the Dragon King to death. The Dragon King meekly returned to Gui Guzi and, admitting what he had done, asked his advice.

Gui Guzi identified the official instructed to carry out the order to execute the Dragon King, then went to see the Chinese terrestrial emperor to persuade him to rescind the order. The emperor was induced by Gui Guzi to challenge the named executioner to a game of chess, during which he would persuade him to request a reprieve from the celestial Jade Emperor. The game continued for some time until the executioner accidentally dropped a chess piece and momentarily closed his eyes. It was known that a soul acts independently during the time when a human is asleep; in this case, the soul of the executioner swiftly returned to heaven, where he carried out the death sentence—the Dragon

King was dead. A few minutes later the emperor broached the subject of a reprieve, but already it was too late.

That night the soul of the Dragon King appeared before the emperor in a dream and, remonstrating with him for failing to obtain a reprieve, asked for retribution. The emperor accompanied the soul of the Dragon King to the Courts of the First and Fifth Judges in the Underworld, where the whole story was explained. The judges settled on a fee for the return to life of the Dragon King, but as the Dragon King had no money with him he had to borrow it from the judges. This he later returned by despatching it from the human world, by burning so-called hell money.[2] This is yet another of the stories to explain the origins of hell money.

Notes

1   It would be interesting to know what was made of the death of the Manchu Emperor, Jia Qing, after he was struck by lightning in 1821.

2   Hell money is the paper currency of the Bank of Hell, usually wads of notes each with an enormous face value but costing a few coppers in terrestrial currency, used by devotees in transactions with the Underworld.

8

Tutelary Gods and the Gods of the Underworld

Cheng Huang

Cheng Huang, the City God, is the tutelary deity of the capital, and of all major walled cities and towns, the spiritual city magistrate responsible to the Jade Emperor in heaven. In imperial China his temple was regarded as the celestial court, or *yamen*, the counterpart to the terrestrial provincial or city *yamen* with its human magistrate, the mandarin responsible to the emperor in Beijing. The City God is well respected and is usually impersonal, but in a number of places and in legend he has been identified locally with various deified humans of the past.

Local city and town mandarins of imperial China combined functions that are today carried out by numerous officials. Formerly, such mandarins were supposed to have exhaustive acquaintance with everything within their jurisdiction, and an unlimited capacity to prevent that which ought to be prevented. Whereas the temporal government controlled the masses by fear of the law, the City God controlled people's morals through the dread of unspeakable punishments after death. Cheng Huang's office is the place where souls of the recently dead are examined, and their records checked to ensure that the correct soul is being sent on in chains to the Courts of the Underworld, there to be judged and purged before being reincarnated, or being sent to the Western Heavens without further ado. Devotees regularly petition the City God on behalf of a deceased to intercede with the Ten Judges in the Underworld.

Tudi Gong

Tudi Gong, the Earth God, and Zao Jun (see Chapter 6), the Kitchen God (God of the Family Stove), were among the most ancient of the deities within the pantheon of popular religion, and certainly date back to pre-Han times.

The ubiquitous local deity of the neighbourhood, Tudi Gong, is the lowest ranking official in the bureaucracy of the celestial pantheon, and is the tutelary deity of each sector of a village or suburb. Individual Tudi Gong occupy the offices of the Earth Gods of the fields, bridges, houses, and mountains, each governing a particular area. Tudi Gong was originally one of the numerous gods of the soil, a personification of the first human resident of a plot of land. Thus in South-East Asia, the Tudi image on the altar of a Chinese immigrant can be portrayed as Malay or Javanese. Each Tudi Gong is looked upon not as a powerful or fearsome deity, but as the protector of the well-being of both town and country dwellers.

Although Earth Gods are almost universally thought to be impersonal spirits—as are the Kitchen Gods, Goddesses of the Bedchamber (or Chuang Mu, revered as an invisible spirit who watches over babies at night, and is invoked when they are sick), and other local community deities—in some areas, mostly in northern and central China, local tradition regards a small number of Earth Gods as the spirits of deceased local worthies.

Dongyue Dadi

In the *Fengshen Yanyi*, Huang Feihu, a warrior prince in his human form, was canonized by Jiang Ziya, and became Dongyue Dadi (Fig. 8.1), the Great Emperor of the Eastern Peak, known also as the Lord of Tai Shan. After many

8.1 Dongyue Dadi, the Great Emperor of the Eastern Peak, is the supreme ruler of the Underworld. He has a very large bureaucratic organization responsible to him for maintaining the register that records the due date on which every living soul must die. Western Hills, Beijing.

colourful adventures during the Shang–Zhou wars, Huang Feihu was appointed the supreme ruler of the Underworld, and the most senior of the Lords of the Five Sacred Peaks of Daoism. Tai Shan in Shandong province, one of these five mountains, has from early times been regarded as an abode of the dead, with the gods who reside there having the bureaucratic function of processing the souls of the deceased.

The very large bureaucratic organization in the Underworld is responsible to Dongyue Dadi for the maintenance of the Book of Life, the register of the due date on which the soul of every living human must die and be summoned to appear before the Ten Judges of the Underworld. The arrest and escort of the soul is carried out by lictors and runners from the *yamen* of the local City Gods. These lictors and runners drag the soul before the City God, together with a report on the soul prepared by the local Earth God, who has carried out a very preliminary interview to ensure that the right person has been arrested (died) and is ready for onward despatch. Again, after verifying the identity of the soul, the City God endorses the Earth God's report, and, if available, adds any further information he might possess on the soul before despatching it under escort to the First Court of the Underworld, where the process of purging the soul of all sin commences.

Ming Fu Shiwang

Although many conflicting ideas exist about the organization of the Underworld, it is generally accepted that there are a total of ten halls or courts, the first and last being administrative. Each is controlled by a judge or king. The overall ruler of the Ten Courts is Yanluo Wang, the Yama (Lord of the Underworld) of Hinduism. Rewards and punishments, including a complex assortment of hells, were elements of Buddhist texts imported into China from India, although in China representation of these subjects was quickly changed to include torture chambers, to conform with Chinese judicial practice. The Ten Presiding Judges, Ming Fu Shiwang, have as their assistants either obsequious scholar-clerks, or bestial gaolers and torturers.

The soul of the deceased arrives in the First Court where the register of names of the living and dead is maintained. It contains details of allotted life spans, along with extracts from reports of the good and evil deeds committed by the soul during life. If the good deeds outweigh the bad, the soul is escorted on to the Tenth Court, also administrative, where the destiny of the soul is decided, that is, whether it is to be despatched straight to the paradise of the Western Heavens, reborn into the world as a human or a creature, or retained in the Underworld as a hungry ghost or a demon gaoler.

The Courts are depicted in gory detail in handbooks of cautionary tales presented to visitors to temples and, more horrific because of the gaudy colours used, on the murals near to or above the images of the Ten Judges. There is an erroneous belief that the judges are bloodthirsty sadists. In fact, the Ten are noted for their mercy, and only send people for punishment because the law requires it. After the soul has passed through all Ten Courts and been fully purged of its sins, and before it is despatched to the human world for rebirth in a new incarnation, it is first anaesthetized with a dish of liquid, often referred to as broth or soup, administered by Grandmother Meng (Meng Po Niangniang) (Fig. 8.2) in her Hall of Oblivion, which causes all memory to be destroyed before rebirth. Once it has been reborn, the soul

8.2 Grandmother Meng in her Hall of Oblivion administers the soup of forgetfulness. This causes all memory to be destroyed before a soul's rebirth back on earth. Temple mural, Taiyuan, Shanxi.

passes out of the jurisdiction of the Lord of Tai Shan and the Ming Fu Shiwang, until the due date for the soul to be summoned by the Underworld lictors comes round yet again.

Taiyi Jiuku Tianzun

Taiyi Jiuku Tianzun, the Great Unity, Deliverer from Suffering, is worshipped all over China as the saviour of sufferers and unfortunates in the Underworld. He is an early orthodox Daoist deity who helps devotees achieve immortality. The title appears to have been created during the Song dynasty by Daoist priests, and today devotees pray to him for longevity and prosperity. Taiyi Jiuku Tianzun is one of the more senior and significant orthodox Daoist deities, a beneficent deity, and one of the Twelve Immortals of Heaven (Shi'er Tianxian) recorded in the *Fengshen Yanyi*. His symbol, a ferocious lion, is often used on temple scrolls to represent his power.

Most devotees claim Taiyi Jiuku Tianzun to be a major Daoist deity of the Big Dipper, the personification of the philosophical concept of the Great Unity, responsible to Yuanshi Tianzun, one of the San Qing Daozu (see Chapter 3), and equal in rank to the Jade Emperor. According to the *Fengshen Yanyi* and other sagas of the gods, he lived during the great era of the Five Sage Rulers of the Legendary Age, also known as the Five Rulers (Wu Di), and was the medical adviser to the Yellow Emperor. Devotees believe Taiyi to be a senior god in charge of lesser, and, in particular, wayward junior gods.

In recent centuries, it has been the view that Taiyi Jiuku Tianzun is the Daoist equivalent of Dizang Wang (Kshitigarbha), the Buddhist Saviour who roams the Underworld seeking and liberating those who repent.

9

Mythical Deities Revealed during the Last Millennium

Hei Di Tianwang

Many mythical deities, such as Hei Di Tianwang (Plate 24), the Heavenly Lord, the Black Emperor, are generally restricted to very local areas and have only been revealed to mankind during the past millennium. The cult of the Heavenly Lord, only present in a rural village temple on the Guangxi–Hunan border, is said to have originated during the reign of the first Ming emperor, Hong Wu (c.1368), when a local minor scholar, reclining on the river bank, heard a pitiful cry for help. A fisherman had just caught a large fish, which appeared to be calling to the scholar to save his life; the fisherman reluctantly threw the fish back into the river. Later that night, the spirit, which had temporarily taken the form of a fish, appeared to the scholar in a dream in its usual semi-human form, and promised to protect the village forever should the villagers build a temple in his honour and revere him. The temple was built and the image of the deity, who had disclosed that he was the Heavenly Lord, the Black Emperor, a celestial being, was prepared in the likeness of the spirit in the dream, with a human body and head, but with the ears of a dog and the snout of a boar, with small tusks.

Wu Xian

Wu Xian, the Five Immortals, otherwise known as the Five Rams, are the patron deities of Guangzhou (Canton). The popular version of their story explains how the five were shepherds who, long ago in what is now Guangzhou, descended from heaven, each wearing a robe of a different colour, and all riding rams. They brought with them the Five Grains that signify plenty. As this is said to have happened about 200 BC, the incident probably alludes to the introduction of grain cultivation to the area. They then turned into five rocks known as the Five Stone Rams, and a supernatural voice speaking out of the clouds claimed that as long as they were worshipped, prosperity would continue. In addition to the five rocks in a temple in Guangzhou, there were five images of mandarins dressed in white, yellow, blue, black, and red, each with ears of rice in their hands in the promise that famine would never strike the city. The temple, Wu Xian Guan, still stands today with several old and battered stone images of rams in the courtyard. The images of the five mandarins, though photographed by a Christian missionary between the World Wars, have long gone.

Qi Sheng Xianniang

Another very localized mythical cult is centred in the small old rural temple at Kwun Hang on Tolo Harbour in the New Territories of Hong Kong, in which reside Qi Sheng Xianniang, the Seven Saintly Immortal Maidens. These deities, whose images stand on the village temple's main altar, have not only protected the villagers, but made a special point of looking after the children who play beside the stream that runs through the hamlet. Local myth explains that once upon a time[1], local fishermen, out casting their nets, only managed to haul in seven perfect and untarnished stones, which they threw back in disgust. Each time they recast their nets the same seven stones were fished out. When eventually it dawned on the fishermen that the stones must have mystical properties, they took them home and placed them in a hut on the hillside. That night the stones glowed with an eerie light, and left the hut of their own accord, floating apparently aimlessly around the countryside until finally they came to rest at the site of the present temple. The fishermen accepted that these stones were from the spirit world and, as the only group of seven they could think of was the Seven Saintly Immortal Maidens, in true Chinese fashion they struck a bargain: we build you a temple, and you protect our interests. Thereafter, water blessed by the Seven has had magical properties and is medicinally potent, especially when a small piece of a tiger skin hanging in the temple is immersed in the water, which is then taken home and boiled. No one nowadays seems to know what became of the stones.

These three examples—the Heavenly Lord, the Five Immortals, and the Seven Saintly Immortal Maidens—are but a few among the innumerable local deities that still exist throughout the length and breadth of China.

Notes

1   The temple keeper claimed to Dr Patrick Hase that this took place some 150 years ago. Dr Hase, a scholar and, at the time of writing, President of the Royal Asiatic Society, Hong Kong Branch, has been researching traditional life in the New Territories for over twenty years.

Chronology

Pre-Creation
The Era of the Three Pure Ones

Creation and Prehistory
Pangu, Creator of the Universe

Legendary Period
The Five Sage Rulers of the Legendary Age:
Fu Xi, Shen Nong, Huang Di, Yao, Shun c.3000–2000 BC

Ancient China

Xia dynasty (founded by Yu)[1]	c.2000–1700 BC
Shang dynasty (also called Yin)	c.1700–1122 BC[2]
Zhou dynasty	1122–256 BC[3]

Imperial China

Qin dynasty	221–207 BC
Han dynasty	206 BC–AD 220
Tang dynasty	618–907
Song dynasty	960–1279
Yuan dynasty	1260–1367
Ming dynasty	1368–1644
Qing dynasty	1644–1911

Republican China   1911–1949

Notes

1 Yao, Shun, and Yu are known as the Three Sage Kings.
2 1122 BC, a popular date of the legendary war leading to the overthrow of the Shang dynasty.
3 Dates before c.850 BC are traditional.

Selected Bibliography

Campbell, Joseph, *Oriental Mythology: The Masks of God*, New York: Viking, 1962.

Ching, Julia, *Chinese Religions*, Basingstoke: The Macmillan Press, 1993.

Christie, Anthony, *Chinese Mythology*, Feltham: Paul Hamlyn, 1968.

Day, Clarence B., *Chinese Peasant Cults*, Taipei: Ch'eng Wen Publishing Co., second edition, 1969.

Doré, Henri, *Recherches sur les Superstitions en Chine*, Shanghai: IIème Partie, 1918.

Du Bose, H. C., *The Dragon, Image and Demon*, London: Partridge & Co., 1886.

Dyson, Verne, *Forgotten Tales of Ancient China*, Shanghai: Commercial Press, 1927.

Garritt, Revd J. C., *Popular Account of the Canonization of the Gods, Illustrated*, Shanghai: Chinese Recorder, April 1899, pp. 162–173.

Geil, William Edgar, *A Yankee on the Yangtze*, London: John Murray, 1902.

Goodrich, Anne Swann, *The Peking Temple of the Eastern Peak*, Nagoya: Monumenta Serica, 1964.

Gray, John Henry, *China*, London: MacMillan, 1878.

Grootaers, Willem, *A Hagiography of the Chinese God Chen-wu*, Nagoya: Folklore Studies 11, 1952.

Hodous, Lewis, *Folkways in China*, London: Arthur Probsthain, 1929.

Howard Smith, D., *Chinese Religions*, London: Weidenfield and Nicolson, 1968.

Kemp, E. G., *The Face of China*, London: 1908.

Lü, Ts'ung-fang, *Chung-kuo Min-chien Chu-shen, Parts 1 and 2* [中國民間諸神（上下冊）; Deities of Chinese Folk Tradition], Taipei: Hsüeh-sheng Shu-chü, 1989.

Palmer, Martin and Zhao Xiaomin, *Essential Chinese Mythology*, London: Thorsons, 1997.

Sanders, Tao Tao, *Dragons, Gods and Spirits from Chinese Mythology*, New York: Peter Lowe, 1980.

Walters, Derek, *Chinese Mythology: An Encyclopedia of Myth and Legend*, London: Aquarian/Thorsons, 1992.

Welch, Holmes, *Taoism: The Parting of the Way*, Boston: Beacon Press, 1957.

Werner, Edward Theodore Chalmers, *Myths and Legends of China*, London: 1922.

_____, *A Dictionary of Chinese Mythology*, Shanghai: Kelly & Walsh Ltd., 1932.

Chinese Gods

Stevens, Keith, *Chinese Gods: The Unseen World of Spirits and Demons*, London: Collins and Brown, 1997.

Index

Bai Di 白帝, White Emperor, 24
Bai Hu 白虎, White Tiger, 23
Bei Di 北帝, Xuantian Shangdi 玄
天上帝, Zhenwu 真武, Northern
Emperor, 3, 18, 19, 20, 21
Beiyou Ji 北遊記 (Journey to the
North), 20
Bixia Yuanjun 碧霞元君, Goddess
of the Azure Clouds, 58

Cang Jie 倉頡, 40, 41
Chang E 嫦娥, Heng E 姮娥,
Goddess of the Moon, 55, 56,
58
Cheng Huang 城隍, City God, 65,
67, 69, 70
Chi You 蚩尤, 41
Chuang Mu 床母, Goddess of the
Bedchamber, 68
Confucius 孔子, 16, 43, 54

Da Ji 妲己, 8, 9, 18
Deng Jiugong *see* Qing Long
Dian Mu 電母, Lightning Matron,
63, 64
Dizang Wang 地藏王, Kshitigarbha,
Buddhist Saviour, 72
Dongwang Mugong 東王木公 ,
Royal Count of the East, 54
Dongyue Dadi 東岳大帝, Lord of
Tai Shan, Supreme Ruler of the
Underworld, Huang Feihu 黃飛
虎, 57, 68, 69, 72
Dragon King(s), *see* Long Wang

Earth God, *see* Tudi
Eight Immortals, 17
Er Lang, *see* Yang Jian
Ershiba Xiuxing 二十八宿星,
Twenty-eight Constellations, 18

Feng Bo, *see* Feng Shen
Feng Shen 風神, Feng Bo 風伯,
Wind God, 61, 63
Fengshen Yanyi 封神演義
(Deification of the Gods), 3, 10,
12, 17, 18, 21, 23, 24, 25, 27, 31,
32, 68, 72
fengshui 風水, 24
Five Immortals, *see* Wu Xian
Five Rams, *see* Wu Xian
Five Sage Rulers, Wu Di 五帝, 35, 72
Fu Xi,
Shen Nong, God of Husbandry
and Agriculture,
Huang Di, Yellow Emperor,
Yao (*see also* Three Sage Kings)
Shun (*see also* Three Sage
Kings)
Fu Xi 伏羲, 31, 32, 35, 36, 38, 39,
see Five Sage Rulers
Fu Xing 福星, Stellar deity of
Happiness and Fortune, *see* San
Xing

Gong Gong 共工, 31
Guan Di 關帝, God of Loyalty, 1
Guan Yin 觀音, Goddess of Mercy,
40, 58,
Gui Guzi 鬼谷子, fortune teller, 65

He Bo 河伯, God of the Yellow
River, 56
Hei Di Tianwang 黑帝天王, 73
Heng and Ha 哼哈二將, Generals
Blower and Snorter, 14, 23, 32
Heng E, *see* Chang E
Hongjun Laozu 洪鈞老子, 25, 26
Hou Yi 后羿, Archer, 56
Houji 后稷, God of Fields and
Crops, Lord of Millet, 60, 61

Houtu 后土, Spirit of the Earth, 59,
Huang Di 黃帝, Yellow Emperor, 6,
38, 39, 40, 41, 42, 60, 72, *see*
Five Sage Rulers
Huang Feihu, *see* Dongyue Dadi

Jade Emperor, *see* Yuhuang
Shangdi
Jiang Ziya 姜子牙, 4, 8, 9, 10, 14,
17, 23, 26, 51, 68
Jiu Tian Xuannü 九天玄女, Dark
Lady of the Ninth Heaven, Nü
Wa 女媧, 30, 31, 32, 36

Kitchen God, *see* Zao Jun
Kshitigarbha, *see* Dizang Wang
Kui Xing 魁星, 16

Laozi 老子, 20, 25, 39, 54, *see also*
Ren Guan, 53
Lei Zu 雷祖, President Board of
Thunder, 63
Lei Gong 雷公, Thunder God, 61,
63, 64
Lei Zhenzi 雷震子, son of Thunder,
63
Leizu 嫘祖, Yuan Fei 元妃, wife of
Yellow Emperor, 39
Li Ji 禮記, *Book of Rites*, 42
Li Jing Tianwang 李靖天王, 11, 12,
13
Li Nazha, *see* Nanzha San Taizi
Lingbao Tianzun 靈寶天尊, High
Pure, *see* San Qing Daozu
Long Wang 龍王, Dragon King(s)
12, 62, 64, 65, 66
Lu Xing 祿星, Stellar deity of
Affluence, Posterity, and
Official Rank, *see* San Xing

Manjusri, *see* Wen Shu Tianjun
Meng Po Niangniang 孟婆娘娘,
Grandmother Meng, 71

Mingfu Shi Wang 冥府十王, Ten
Presiding Judges in Courts of
the Underworld, *see* Underworld
Mo Wang 魔王, Demon King, 20
Monkey King, *see* Sun Wukong

Nanji Tianzun 南極天尊, Old
Immortal of the South Pole, *see*
Shouxing
Nazha San Taizi 哪吒三太子, Li
Nazha 李哪吒, Third Prince, 12,
13, 23
Northern Emperor, *see* Bei Di
Nü Wa, *see* Jiu Tian Xuannü

Pangu 盤古, 28, 29, *see* Di Guan
(San Guan Dadi)
Patriarch Peng 彭祖, *see* Shou Xing

Qi Sheng Niangniang 七聖娘娘,
Seven Saintly Immortal
Maidens, 74
Qi Xiannü 七仙女, Seventh Maid,
Weaving Girl, 52
Qing Long 青龍, Blue Dragon,
Deng Jiugong 鄧九公, 23
Qitian Da Sheng, *see* Sun Wukong

Ren Guan, *see* San Guan
Ren Huang, *see* San Guan

Sakyamuni Buddha, 54
San Guan Dadi 三官大帝, 28, 52
    Tian Guan 天官, Tian Huang 天
    皇, Ruler or Emperor of
    Heaven, 28, 53
    Di Guan 地官, Di Huang 地皇,
    Emperor of the Earth, 28,
    53, 61
    Shui Guan 水官, Ruler of the
    Waters, or Ren Guan 人官,
    Ren Huang 人皇, Emperor of
    Mankind, 28, 53

San Qing Daozu 三清道祖, Three Pure Ones, 26, 72
    Yuanshi Tianzun, Lingbao Tianzun and Shenbao Tianzun

San Xing 三星, The Three Stellar Gods of the most desirable blessings, 57, 58
    see Fu Xing, Lu Xing, and Shou Xing

Sanshiliu Tianjiang 三十六天將, 19

Seven Saintly Immortal Maidens, *see* Qi Sheng Niangniang

Seventh Maid, *see* Qi Xiannü

Shan Shen 山神, Spirit of the Mountain, 32,

Shang Di 上帝, Supreme Emperor, God, 34 note 2, 49

Sheji 社稷, God of the Harvest, Soil, and Grain, 60,

Shen Nong 神農, 36, 37, 38, 39, 40, *see* Di Guan

Shen Nong Bencao Jing 神農本草經 (Shen Nong Pharmacopoeia), 42 note 3

Shenbao Tianzun 神寶天尊, Supreme Pure, *see* San Qing Daozu

Shou Laoren 壽老人, 56

Shou Xing 壽星, Nanji Tianzun, Stellar deity of Longevity, 42, 57, *see* San Xing

Shui Guan, *see* San Guan

Shun 舜, 43, 44, 45, 47, 48, 60

Sun Wukong 孫悟空, Qitian Da Sheng 齊天大聖, Monkey King, 5, 10, 15, 55

Tai Sui 太歲, Yin Jiao 殷郊, Yin Tianjun 殷天君, President Celestial Ministry of Time, 16, 17, 18

Taibai Jinxing 太白金星, 24

Taiyang Xingjun 太陽星君, Lord of Yang, God of the Sun, 33

Taiyi Jiuku Tianzun 太乙救苦天尊, Great Unity, Daoist Saviour in Underworld, 13, 72

Taiyi Zhenren 太乙真人, 13, 14

Taiyin Xingjun 太陰星君, Lady of the Yin, Goddess of the Moon, 33

Third Prince, *see* Nazha San Taizi

Three Sage Kings 43, *see* Yao, Shun and Yu

Tian Fei 天妃, 18

Tudi 土地, Tudi Gong 土地公, tutelary Earth God, 60, 68, 70

Twenty-four Heavenly Generals, 11

Underworld, 50,
    Courts of, 51, 66, 67, 69, 70, 71, 72, Mingfu Shi Wang, *see also* Yanluo Wang

Vaisravana, 13

Weaving Girl and Cowherd, 52, *see* Qi Xiannü

Wen Chang Dijun 文昌帝君, 16

Wenshu Tianzun 文殊天尊, Manjusri, 13

Wu Di 五帝, *see* Five Sage Rulers

Wu Xian 五仙, Five Immortals, Five Rams, 73

Xi Wangmu 西王母, Queen Mother of the West, 53, 54, 56

Xiyou Ji 西遊記 (Journey to the West), 5, 20

Xuantan Yuanshuai, *see* Zhao Gongming

Xuantian Shangdi, *see* Bei Di

Xuanzang 玄奘, 5

Yaksha, 12

Yang Jian 楊戩, Er Lang 二郎, 3, 10, 14

Yanluo Wang 閻羅王, Ruler of Ten Courts of the Underworld, 70

Yao 堯, 43, 44, 45, 48, see Three Sage Kings and Five Sage Rulers

Yellow Emperor, see Huang Di

Yin Jiao, see Tai Sui

Yu 禹, 43, 46, 47, 48, see Three Sage Kings

Yu Huang Dadi 玉皇大帝, Jade Emperor, 7, 9, 12, 18, 19, 20, 22, 24, 27, 49, 50, 51, 53, 54, 64, 72 see also Tian Guan

Yu Shen 雨神, Yu Shi 雨師, Rain God, 61, 62

Yu Shi, see Yu Shen

Yuan Fei, see Leizu

Yuanshi Tianzun 元始天尊, Jade Pure, 9, 26, 27, 72, see San Qing Laozu

Yuexia Laoren 月下老人, Old Man of the Moon, 57

Zao Jun 灶君, Kitchen God, 51, 52, 68

Zhang Denglai 張等來, 51

Zhao Gongming 趙公明, Xuantan Yuanshuai 玄壇元帥, Marshal of the Dark Altar, General of the White Tiger, 21, 22

Zhen Wu, see Bei Di

Zhou Xin (Zhou Wang) 紂辛, 8, 9, 14, 17, 18, 26, 31, 32

Zhu Rong 祝融, God of Fire, 42

MAP OF CHINA